ADVANCED MODULAR MATHEMATICS

Pure Mathematics
1

for A and AS level

The University of London modular mathematics syllabus

National Extension College Trust

NATIONAL
EXTENSION
COLLEGE

Collins Educational

An Imprint of HarperCollinsPublishers

Published by Collins Educational
An imprint of HarperCollins*Publishers*
77–85 Fulham Palace Road
Hammersmith
London W6 8JB

© National Extension College Trust Ltd 1994
First published 1994
Reprinted 1995
ISBN 0 00 322394 9

This book was written by Stephen Webb for the National Extension College Trust Ltd.
Stephen Webb asserts the moral right to be identified as the author of this work.

Designed by Derek Lee
Cover design and implementation by Derek Lee
Page layout by Mary Bishop
Project editor, Hugh Hillyard-Parker

The author and publishers thank Pat Perkins and Joan Billington for their comments on this book.

Printed and bound in the UK by Scotprint Ltd, Musselburgh.

The National Extension College is an educational trust and a registered charity with a distinguished body of trustees. It is an independent, self-financing organisation.

Since it was established in 1963, NEC has pioneered the development of flexible learning for adults. NEC is actively developing innovative materials and systems for distance-learning options from basic skills and general education to degree and professional training.

For further details of NEC resources that support *Advanced Modular Mathematics*, and other NEC courses, contact NEC Customer Services:

National Extension College Trust Ltd
18 Brooklands Avenue
Cambridge CB2 2HN
Telephone 0223 316644, Fax 0223 313586

CONTENTS

P1

Advanced Modular Mathematics

This book is one of a series covering the University of London Examination and Assessment Council's modular 'A' level Mathematics syllabus. It covers all the subject material for Pure Mathematics 1 (Module P1).

While this series of text books has been structured to match the University of London (ULEAC) syllabuses, we hope that the informal style of the text and approach to important concepts will encourage other readers, whose final examinations are from other examination Boards, to use the books for extra reading and practice.

This book is meant to be *used*: read the text, study the worked examples and work through the exercises, which will give you practice in the basic skills you need for maths at this level. There are many books for advanced mathematics, which include many more exercises: use this book to direct your studies, making use of as many other resources as you can. This book will act as a bridge between your new syllabus and the many older books that can still give even more practice in advanced mathematics.

Exercises are given at the end of each section; these range from the basic to exam-type questions. Many exercises, and worked examples, are based on *applications* of the mathematics in this book. We have given answers to all problems, so that you can check your work.

The National Extension College has more experience of flexible-learning materials than any other body. This series is a distillation of that experience: *Advanced Modular Mathematics* helps to put you in control of your own learning.

1

Algebra

INTRODUCTION
You will probably already be familiar with many of the basic techniques in algebra from the work you have done up to now. In this course, it is extremely important that you master these, and others that you will meet along the way, so that you're not hindered later when this ability is taken for granted. The section describes how to factorise algebraic expressions, combine and simplify algebraic fractions and divide polynomials by a linear factor.

Polynomials

A polynomial is a collection of terms involving a variable, like $x^3 - 2x^2 + 5$ or simply $3x + 1$. When the highest power of the variable is 2, for example, $x^2 - 3x + 7$, it is called a *quadratic* polynomial, or quadratic for short. A *cubic* polynomial, like $x^3 - 4x^2 + 5x + 4$, has a highest power of 3. As you can see, polynomials are usually written with the term involving the highest power first, then the powers go down until the term without the variable called the *constant* term.

We can label polynomials by giving them a letter and writing $f(x)$ or $g(x)$ if our variable is x, so that we could write our cubic polynomial above as:

$$f(x) \quad = \quad x^3 - 4x^2 + 5x + 4$$

The variable is not always x – it can sometimes be another letter, t say, in which case our cubic would be written as:

$$f(t) \quad = \quad t^3 - 4t^2 + 5t + 4$$

Once we've labelled the polynomial like this, we can simply write $f(x)$ instead of writing it down in full when we need to refer to it. Now we can take another polynomial, our quadratic above for example, and call it $g(x)$, so that:

$$g(x) \quad = \quad x^2 - 3x + 7$$

Adding and subtracting polynomials

If we want to add the polynomials, $f(x) + g(x)$, we add the like terms together, so that the x^2 terms are added together, and so on. For the moment, we can set this sum out as though we were adding numbers, although normally you would write them on one line:

$$f(x) \qquad\qquad x^3 - 4x^2 + 5x + 4$$
$$+\, g(x) \qquad\qquad \underline{x^2 - 3x + 7}$$
$$x^3 - 3x^2 + 2x + 11$$

We use the same method, of combining like terms, when it comes to subtracting polynomials, but we have to be *very* careful to watch the signs. Probably the best way until you're very confident is to take the subtraction in stages. Suppose you want to subtract $g(x)$ from $f(x)$. You could write:

$$f(x) - g(x) = (x^3 - 4x^2 + 5x + 4) - (x^2 - 3x + 7)$$

Since there is nothing outside the first bracket on the right-hand side we don't need it and we can write the polynomial without it. The last bracket has a negative sign outside and this means that *all* the signs have to be changed if we want to remove it. When this has been done, we add the like terms together as we did when we added the polynomials:

$$\begin{aligned} f(x) - g(x) &= x^3 - 4x^2 + 5x + 4 - x^2 + 3x - 7 \\ &= x^3 - 5x^2 + 8x - 3 \end{aligned}$$

You should now be able to answer Exercise 1 on p. 8.

Multiplying polynomials

You will probably already be familiar with multiplying polynomials in certain cases – for example:

$$\begin{aligned} (3x - 2)\,(2x + 5) &= 6x^2 + 15x - 4x - 10 \\ &= 6x^2 + 11x - 10 \end{aligned}$$

It's worthwhile practising this until you can write the product straight down. In the previous example, it's quite easy to see the x^2-term and the constant term because they are the first two and last two terms multiplied together. To find the x-term, you have to multiply the outer two together and the inner two together and add these:

$$-2 \times 2x = -4x$$

$$(3x - 2)\,(2x + 5) \qquad -4x + 15x = 11x$$

$$3x \times 5 = 15x$$

When multiplying more complicated polynomials, you need to be quite systematic. Suppose we had to find the product of two quadratics, for example:

$$(1 - 3x + x^2)\,(1 - 4x - x^2)$$

One way would be to multiply everything in the right-hand bracket by each of the terms in the left-hand bracket in turn, and then collect like terms together:

$$(1 - 3x + x^2)(1 - 4x - x^2) = \underbrace{1 - 4x - x^2} \quad \underbrace{-3x + 12x^2 + 3x^3} \quad \underbrace{+x^2 - 4x^3 - x^4}$$

$$= 1 - 7x + 12x^2 - x^3 - x^4$$

You should now be able to answer Exercises 2 and 3 on p. 8.

Adding and subtracting fractions

We have become so used to finding values with the help of our calculators, which work mainly with decimals, that we tend to forget how to 'do' fractions. It's a pity this happens, because algebraic fractions work in much the same way as arithmetic fractions and it's *very* useful to be confident in dealing with either of these. Compare these two sums, for instance:

1) $\quad \dfrac{3}{8} + \dfrac{2}{5}$

2) $\quad \dfrac{2}{3x + 1} + \dfrac{1}{x - 3}$

It is easy to see why we would normally want to simplify the first expression – to make it easier to deal with – and how we would do this. With a little thought, we can see we will often want to do the same with the second expression. At first sight there doesn't seem to be much connection between them, but in fact the method used to combine them is the same. For (1) we find the lowest common denominator, the smallest number that is exactly divisible by both 8 and 5. Since these two numbers have no factors in common, this is just 8×5. Putting this at the bottom of the fraction:

$$\dfrac{\overline{}}{8 \times 5}$$

we take each separate fraction in turn and see what the denominator has to be multiplied by to give the common denominator. For the first fraction, the denominator 8 has to be multiplied by 5 to give the common denominator, 8×5, so it is by 5 that we multiply the figure at the top, in this case 3. Similarly, for the second fraction, we multiply the 2 by 8, giving altogether:

$$\frac{3}{8} + \frac{2}{5} = \frac{(5 \times 3) + (8 \times 2)}{8 \times 5} = \frac{31}{40}$$

Using the same procedure, we can combine the two algebraic fractions in (2):

$$\frac{2}{3x + 1} + \frac{1}{x - 3} = \frac{(x - 3) \times 2 + (3x + 1) \times 1}{(3x + 1)(x - 3)}$$

3

Multiplying out the brackets we can now simplify the numerator (the top part of the fraction):

$$= \frac{2x - 6 + 3x + 1}{(3x + 1)(x - 3)}$$

$$= \frac{5x - 5}{(3x + 1)(x - 3)}$$

Note that we don't multiply out the two factors on the bottom (the denominator) – there's no particular advantage in doing this.

Let's try another pair:

3) $\quad \dfrac{3}{8} + \dfrac{7}{16}$

4) $\quad \dfrac{3}{x + 1} + \dfrac{5}{(x + 1)^2}$

To combine the fractions in (3), it's only necessary to take 16 as the common denominator, since 8 divides into this exactly. We have to multiply 8 by 2 to give 16, but the second fraction remains unchanged:

$$\frac{3}{8} + \frac{7}{16} = \frac{(2 \times 3) + 7}{16} = \frac{13}{16}$$

Similarly, in (4) the common denominator will be $(x + 1)^2$:

$$\frac{3}{x + 1} + \frac{5}{(x + 1)^2} = \frac{(x + 1) \times 3 + 5}{(x + 1)^2}$$

$$= \frac{3x + 3 + 5}{(x + 1)^2} = \frac{3x + 8}{(x + 1)^2}$$

Exactly the same process applies if we are subtracting fractions, but this time we have to watch signs very carefully. With algebraic fractions, write the extra factors in brackets and remove the brackets in two stages until you've had a bit of practice.

Let's try an example of this:

$$\frac{x - 1}{1 - 2x} - \frac{x + 1}{1 + 2x} = \frac{(1 + 2x)(x - 1) - (1 - 2x)(x + 1)}{(1 - 2x)(1 + 2x)}$$

$$= \frac{(x - 1 + 2x^2 - 2x) - (x + 1 - 2x^2 - 2x)}{(1 - 2x)(1 + 2x)}$$

$$= \frac{x - 1 + 2x^2 - 2x - x - 1 + 2x^2 + 2x}{(1 - 2x)(1 + 2x)}$$

$$= \frac{4x^2 - 2}{(1 - 2x)(1 + 2x)} = \frac{4x^2 - 2}{1 - 4x^2}$$

Note that in this case we *have* multiplied out the two factors in the denominator because they happen to give a neat product, the *difference of two squares.* While we're on this subject, make sure you can recognise this form and know how it can be factorised. Here are some examples:

$$x^2 - 16 = (x - 4)(x + 4)$$
$$y^2 - 1 = (y - 1)(y + 1)$$
$$4p^2 - q^2 = (2p - q)(2p + q)$$
$$25r^2 - 16s^2 = (5r - 4s)(5r + 4s) \text{ etc}$$

You should now be able to answer Exercise 4 on p. 9.

Factorising quadratics

Suppose we have to factorise $x^2 + 7x + 12$, which means expressing it in the form $(x + a)(x + b)$ where a and b are numbers we have to find. If we multiply these brackets out, giving $x^2 + (a + b)x + ab$ and compare the quadratics, we can see that we want to choose a and b so that $ab = 12$ and $a + b = 7$. This is not difficult: one must be 3, the other 4 and the factors are $(x + 3)(x + 4)$. Note that if the original expression had been $x^2 - 7x + 12$, we would still have $ab = 12$ but now $a + b = -7$. Since the product ab is positive, the numbers a and b have the same signs, as the sum $a + b$ is negative, they must both be negative and so the factors in this case would be $(x - 3)(x - 4)$.

If ab is negative, a and b have opposite signs. Then we have to look at the sum $a + b$, the x-coefficient. If this is positive, the larger of a and b is positive: if negative, the larger is negative. So for example with $x^2 + 2x - 8$: $ab = -8$ means that a and b have opposite signs. $a + b = 2$, so the larger is positive: $+4, -2$ with factors $(x + 4)(x - 2)$. With $x^2 - x - 12$: $ab = -12$, again opposite signs but this time the larger is negative: $-4, +3$ with factors $(x - 4)(x + 3)$.

We have to use a slightly different method when the coefficient of x^2 is not 1. Maybe you already have a way of doing this which works for you – fine! Just make sure that you can do the practice examples without too much trouble. Otherwise, here is one way – there are many others.

Suppose we have to factorise, for example, $2x^2 + 11x + 12$. We're still looking for two numbers a and b, but this time the product ab is the product of the x^2–coefficient and the constant, i.e. $ab = 2 \times 12 = 24$. The sum, $a + b$ is 11 as before. The two numbers are 8 and 3 but instead of fitting straight into the brackets, we add an x to each. They are then the outer and inner products:

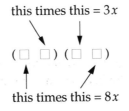

this times this $= 3x$

$(\square \ \ \square)(\square \ \ \square)$

this times this $= 8x$

We now have to look at the given quadratic – since the x^2–coefficient is 2, one of the x-coefficients must be 2 and the other 1, and the $2x$ must be part of the product $8x$:

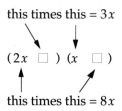

We can now fill in the other figures:

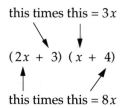

One more example: $3x^2 + 10x - 8$. We're looking for two numbers a and b such that $ab = 3 \times -8 = -24$ and $a + b = 10$. The sum is negative and the product positive, so a and b have different signs, and the larger is positive; this gives us $+12$ and -2:

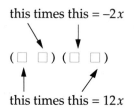

The x^2-coefficient is 3, so it must be $3x$ and x, with $3x$ part of the product $12x$:

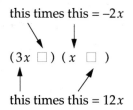

Then we can write down the factors $(3x - 2)(x + 4)$.

You should now be able to answer Exercises 5 and 6 on p. 9.

Squaring linear functions

When we think about a quadratic function, we would normally imagine an expression consisting of terms with x^2, x and constants, something like:

$$f(x) \quad = \quad 3x^2 - 4x + 5,$$

which is the standard form of a quadratic function. If we take an expression like this and rearrange it, we can rewrite it in such a way that we can immediately extract more information about the function. This process of rearranging the expression is called *completing the square* – but before we start let's make sure we are quite proficient at writing down the squares of linear functions like $x + 5$ and $2x - 3$.

You double the constant for the x-coefficient and square the constant for the new constant, so that:

$$(x + 5)^2 \quad = \quad x^2 + 10x + 25$$
$$(x - 3)^2 \quad = \quad x^2 - 6x + 9$$

And when the coefficient of x is not 1, you double the product of this term and the constant for the new x-term, so that:

Mentally, $\qquad 2 \times 2x \times 3 \qquad = \quad 12x$

$\qquad\qquad\qquad (2x + 3)^2 \qquad = \quad 4x^2 + 12x + 9$

Mentally, $\qquad 2 \times 3x \times (-4) \quad = \quad -24x$

and $\qquad\qquad (3x - 4)^2 \qquad = \quad 9x^2 - 24x + 16$

It's important to learn to do these automatically as you'll find it saves you a lot of time and will help you with what follows.

Completing the square

Suppose we take quite a simple quadratic function, say:

$$f(x) \quad = \quad x^2 + 4x + 5$$

and try and find a linear function whose square is $f(x)$. We can see that this is not quite possible – although the square of $x + 2$ is close,

$$(x + 2)^2 \quad = \quad x^2 + 4x + 4$$

but we need to add 1 to give $f(x)$. Similarly, if we took another function,

$$g(x) \qquad = \quad x^2 - 6x + 6$$

the square of $x - 3$ is close,

$$(x - 3)^2 \quad = \quad x^2 - 6x + 9$$

but now we would have to subtract 3 from this to give $g(x)$. Let's look at these two examples:

$$f(x) \quad = \quad x^2 + 4x + 5 \quad = \quad (x + 2)^2 + 1$$
$$g(x) \quad = \quad x^2 - 6x + 6 \quad = \quad (x - 3)^2 - 3$$

You can see that the constant in the bracket is chosen to be half of the x-coefficient in the standard form, so that the coefficients of x^2 and x are correct. An adjustment then has to be made to the square of this constant so that we have the constant in the standard form. For example:

$$h(x) = x^2 - 8x + 25$$

halve the x-coefficient, which gives -4, so the bracket is $(x-4)^2$. This gives $x^2 - 8x + 16$, so we have to add 9 to get $h(x)$:

$$h(x) \quad = \quad x^2 - 8x + 25 \quad = \quad (x-4)^2 + 9$$

If the coefficient of x^2 is something other than 1, we can make the working easier if we rearrange the quadratic first of all. For example, if $f(x) = 2x^2 + 8x + 7$, we take the coefficient of the x^2-term, which is 2, out of the first two terms: $f(x) = 2(x^2 + 4x) + 7$. We then complete the square for the expression in the bracket: $f(x) = 2[(x + 2)^2 - 4] + 7$ and finally remove the square bracket:

$$f(x) \quad = \quad 2(x + 2)^2 - 8 + 7 \quad = \quad 2(x + 2)^2 - 1$$

Similarly if the coefficient of x^2 is negative:

$$
\begin{aligned}
g(x) \quad &= \quad 4 - 6x - 3x^2 \\
&= \quad 4 - 3[x^2 + 2x] \qquad \text{(remember to change the sign} \\
&= \quad 4 - 3[(x + 1)^2 - 1)] \qquad \text{of the } x\text{-term)} \\
&= \quad 4 - 3(x + 1)^2 + 3 \\
&= \quad 7 - 3(x + 1)^2
\end{aligned}
$$

You should now be able to complete Exercises 7, 8 and 9 on p. 9.

EXERCISES

1 If $\quad f(x) \quad = \quad 2x^3 - x^2 + 7x - 11$

$\qquad g(x) \quad = \quad x^3 + 4x^2 - x - 1$

$\qquad h(x) \quad = \quad 2x^2 - x - 5$

find **a** $f(x) + g(x)$ **b** $f(x) + h(x)$ **c** $f(x) - g(x)$ **d** $g(x) - h(x)$

2 *Write down* the following products:

a $(x + 1)(x + 9)$ **b** $(x + 3)(x + 5)$ **c** $(x - 3)(x + 4)$

d $(x + 6)(x - 2)$ **e** $(x - 3)(x - 2)$ **f** $(x - 1)(x - 5)$ **g** $(2x + 1)(x + 1)$

h $(3x + 2)(x + 2)$ **i** $(3x - 1)(x + 1)$ **j** $(2x - 1)(2x + 1)$

k $(3x - 1)(2x - 3)$ **l** $(4x + 3)(2x - 3)$

3 Find the products:

a $(1 - 2x)(1 - 5x - 7x^2)$ **b** $(3 - x - 2x^2)(2 - 3x + 4x^2)$

4 Express the following as a single fraction, simplifying as far as possible.

a $\dfrac{1}{x+2}+\dfrac{1}{x+3}$ **b** $\dfrac{2}{x+3}-\dfrac{1}{x+4}$ **c** $\dfrac{1}{x-5}-\dfrac{1}{x-4}$

d $\dfrac{x+2}{x-2}-\dfrac{x-2}{x+2}$ **e** $\dfrac{3}{x-3}+\dfrac{2x}{(x-3)^2}$ **f** $\dfrac{3}{x-3}+\dfrac{2x}{x^2-9}$

5 Find the factors of

a x^2+5x+6 **b** x^2+2x-8 **c** x^2-x-20 **d** $x^2-11x+30$

e $a^2-7a+10$ **f** $b^2+10b+24$ **g** $y^2-9y+20$ **h** $p^2-7p-18$

i* x^3+x^2-6x **j*** x^3+3x^2-40x

*Take out the factor of x first of all.

6 Find the factors of

a $3x^2-16x+5$ **b** $2x^2-5x-3$ **c** $5x^2-2x-7$ **d** $6x^2-13x+6$

7 Try to write down:

a $(x+2)^2$ **b** $(x-4)^2$ **c** $(x+\tfrac{1}{2})^2$ **d** $(x+\tfrac{2}{3})^2$ **e** $(2x+1)^2$

f $(3x+5)^2$ **g** $(2x-7)^2$ **h** $(x+a)^2$ **i** $(bx+c)^2$ **j** $(px-q)^2$

8 Complete the square for:

a x^2+2x+4 **b** x^2+8x-4 **c** x^2-4x+1 **d** $x^2-10x+20$

e x^2+x+1 **f** x^2-3x-4

9 Complete the square for:

a $2x^2-8x+5$ **b** $3x^2+10x+3$ **c** $8-8x-x^2$ **d** $6+5x-2x^2$

(handwritten) $f(x)=2x^2+8x+7$

(handwritten) $(2x^2+8x)+7$

(handwritten) $(x+4x)$ $2(x^2-4x)+5$

(handwritten) $2(x+2)^2 \quad \tfrac{3}{2}2(x^2-\tfrac{8}{4}x)^2 \cdot -8+5$

SUMMARY

This section dealt with fundamental techniques you will be using throughout the course: they come into the solution of virtually every question. The key is probably accuracy in even the smallest detail. If you do tend to make a mistake with a certain operation, try making a note of it so that you become less and less liable to that particular kind of slip.

SECTION

2

Functions

INTRODUCTION This section introduces the idea of two variables related to each other by some rule and how this relationship can be written in a standard and precise form, called a function. We shall then look at particular types of functions, how they can be combined and turned round. Finally we will look at graphs as a different way of expressing the relationship between two variables and the effect that slight changes in the function have upon these graphs.

Transforming numbers

To get the idea of a function, imagine you are sitting in front of a computer which is displaying 'Guess my rule!' on its screen. It's inviting you to play a game where you tap a number into the computer, it changes this number according to an unknown rule it has 'chosen' and then shows you the result. After several attempts, you can then try and guess the rule which the computer is using to transform your numbers.

Let's suppose you decide to play and your first choice of number is 5 – the computer responds with 14. When you choose 3 the computer produces 8 in reply and –2 gives –7. Can you begin to guess the rule? Probably not at this stage, it's not so obvious. Choosing 0 is usually a good move – if part of the rule is to add or subtract a number, this choice finds the number immediately. In this case the computer answers '–1', so the rule probably includes subtracting 1. Then choose a number next to one of your other numbers – this can give you, by the difference in the responses, the factor by which the numbers are multiplied. Choosing 6 gives 17, which is 3 more than the answer for 5. An increase of 1 on your side produces an increase of 3 on the computer's side. Putting these two pieces of information together, you guess that the rule is 'multiply the number by 3 and subtract 1'. You can see that this rule does in fact give you the answers that were given.

We call this rule a *function* and to write it mathematically, we first of all give it a name – or at least a letter. Functions are often given the letters f, g or h, so we'll call it 'f'. Now we have to describe what the function does, so we put a letter to represent the number chosen (this is usually x) and by the side put what this letter would be transformed to using the rule. For f, the function we've just been looking at, we would write:

$$f: \quad x \quad \mapsto \quad 3x - 1$$

or, as an equation, $f(x) = 3x - 1$. Then we could calculate the result of putting 5 in by:

$$
\begin{aligned}
f(5) &= 3 \times 5 - 1 &= 14 &\quad \text{and putting 3 in by} \\
f(3) &= 3 \times 3 - 1 &= 8 &\quad \text{and putting } -2 \text{ in by} \\
f(-2) &= (3 \times -2) - 1 = &-7 &
\end{aligned}
$$

If the computer had chosen a different rule, say 'square the number and add two', we can call this function 'g' and write:

$$g: \quad x \quad \mapsto \quad x^2 + 2$$

or, using the equation notation, $g(x) = x^2 + 2$.

You should now be able to answer Exercises 1, 2 and 3 on p. 28.

Domain

If we look at the following function

$$r: \quad x \quad \mapsto \quad 2\sqrt{x}$$

we can see that it's not quite the same as the other functions. (Remember that $\sqrt{x}$ means that we take the *positive* square root of x.) With the rest, it doesn't matter what number is chosen for the left-hand side – something sensible appears on the right. With r, some choices still produce reasonable answers – putting 4 instead of x gives 4 back and 25 gives 10 in reply, for instance. The trouble starts if we have a *negative* value of x, say -4. Then the right-hand side becomes $2\sqrt{-4}$ and there are no real numbers whose square is -4. Only *positive* numbers give a real result, so our choice of x is *limited*. We warn possible users of the function of this fact by putting the set of values to which x is restricted after the description of the rule, in this case:

$$r: \quad x \quad \mapsto \quad 2\sqrt{x} \; ; \quad x \geq 0$$

This set of values is called the '*domain*' of the function r.

Range

The set of values which is produced by the right-hand side can also be limited. If we have another look at the function we called g:

$$g: \quad x \quad \mapsto \quad x^2 + 2$$

we can see that since x^2 is always greater than or equal to zero, $x^2 + 2 \geq 2$ for any value of x. The set of values taken by the transformed numbers is called the '*range*' of the function (g in this case).

You should now be able to answer Exercise 4 on pp. 28–29.

Functions

Let's go back to our first function:

$$f: \quad x \quad \mapsto \quad 3x - 1.$$

Any value that we choose for x is transformed to a unique value. So, given a value after the transformation, we can find the only value of x from which this could have come. As an example, 3 goes to 8 and no other value of x would be transformed to 8. In this case, we call the function *'one to one'*, written 1–1. A picture can show this:

Figure 2.1

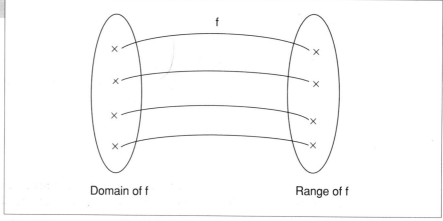

Domain of f   Range of f

Not all functions are 1–1. If we look again at the function g, for example, we find that different values can produce the same answer:

$$g: \quad x \quad \mapsto \quad x^2 + 2$$
$$g(3) \quad = \quad 3^2 + 2 = 11$$
$$g(-3) \quad = \quad (-3)^2 + 2 = 11$$

Figure 2.2

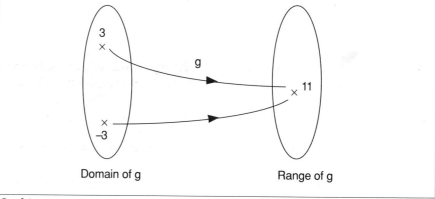

Domain of g   Range of g

In this case, g is *not* 1–1; we call it 'many to one'.

You should now be able to answer Exercise 5 on p. 29.

Inverses of functions

Assume we have a simple function, V such that:

$$\text{V}: \quad x \quad \mapsto \quad 2x + 1$$

You can check that $\text{V}(2) = 5$ and $\text{V}(7) = 15$. The *inverse* of the function V is another function that tells us what value of x we have to put into V to produce a given number. For example, what value of x gives $\text{V}(x) = 11$?

It must be 5, because $\text{V}(5) = 11$. Since the function is quite uncomplicated we can probably work out x given any value of $\text{V}(x)$.

For example,

if $\text{V}(x) = 23$, x must be 11

if $\text{V}(x) = -5$, x must be -3.

So what is the rule that transforms $\text{V}(x)$ to x? If we look, we can see that it is

'subtract 1 and halve the result'.

Writing this as a function, which we call V^{-1},

$$\text{V}^{-1}: \quad x \quad \mapsto \quad \frac{x-1}{2}$$

For a function like this, we can see what the inverse function must be without too much difficulty. We need a more systematic approach to use when they become more complicated, however.

To find the inverse function, we call the result of the transformation y. For example, if:

$$\text{w}: \quad x \quad \mapsto \quad 4x - 12,$$

then we put $y = 4x - 12$. Having done this we put x *in terms of y*. In this case we would have:

$$y + 12 \ = \ 4x$$

$$x \quad \ = \ \frac{y}{4} + 3$$

Then the expression for x is the right-hand side of the inverse function, only we replace the y by an x as we start with an x on the left, i.e.:

$$\text{w}^{-1}: x \quad \mapsto \quad \frac{x}{4} + 3$$

So, $\quad \text{w}^{-1}(8) = \dfrac{8}{4} + 3 = 5$, and $\text{w}(5) = 4 \times 5 - 12 = 8$

Figure 2.3

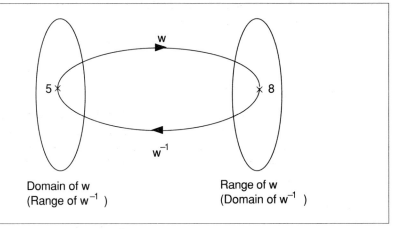

Domain of w
(Range of w^{-1})

Range of w
(Domain of w^{-1})

Since the inverse function w^{-1} starts off from the right-hand side, its domain is the *range of w*. Similarly, since it ends up on the left-hand side, its range is the *domain of w*.

Let's have a look at a slightly different type of function – (since we're running out of letters we'll start back at the beginning again and call this f).

$$f: \quad x \quad \mapsto \quad \frac{x+1}{x-1}; \quad x \neq 1$$

Note the restriction on the domain. This is because when $x = 1$ the bottom of the fraction would have the value of zero, which is not allowed. To find the inverse function f^{-1}, we set:

$$y \quad = \quad \frac{x+1}{x-1}$$

Now comes a trick which you'll be using later for another topic. To express x in terms of y, we cross multiply:

$$y(x-1) \quad = \quad x+1$$
$$yx - y \quad = \quad x+1$$

then collect any terms containing x on one side, any other terms to the other:

$$yx - x \quad = \quad 1+y$$

then take out the factor of x from the left-hand side:

$$x(y-1) \quad = \quad y+1$$

i.e. $$x \quad = \quad \frac{y+1}{y-1}$$

So we can write the inverse function f^{-1} as:

$$f^{-1}: \quad x \quad \mapsto \quad \frac{x+1}{x-1}; \quad x \neq 1$$

Does this sound familiar? It's exactly the same as f. In this case we say that f is a *self-inverse* function.

You should now be able to answer Exercise 6 on p. 29.

Restriction on domain

Sometimes we have to restrict the domain of a function in order to ensure that it's 1–1. The point is that a function can't be many to one and have an inverse, otherwise you would have a single value being transformed to more than one possible value and a function is not allowed to be one to many.

Figure 2.4

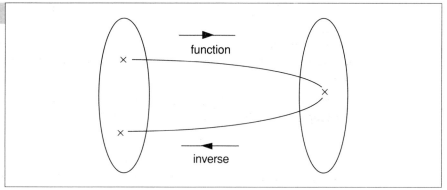

An example would be:

$$m: \quad x \quad \mapsto \quad x^2$$

with an inverse function:

$$m^{-1}: x \quad \mapsto \quad \sqrt{x}$$

The domain of m has to be restricted to the *non-negative* reals, which is the same as the domain of m^{-1}. When the two functions are written as

$$m: x \quad \mapsto \quad x^2 \,;\, x \geq 0, \qquad m^{-1}: x \mapsto \sqrt{x} \,;\, x \geq 0,$$

there is a 1–1 correspondence between the elements in the two domains. When we come to some of the trigonometric functions and their inverses, you'll find that the domain is quite often narrowed down to a little section to ensure this 1–1 condition.

Composition of functions

We've actually already done this, although you may not have noticed. Anything like

$$w: \quad x \quad \mapsto \quad 4x - 12$$

can be looked on as the *composition* of the two functions,

$$w_1 : \quad x \quad \longmapsto \quad 4x$$

$$w_2 : \quad x \quad \longmapsto \quad x - 12$$

We'll get different results according to which of these two we take first, so *order is important*. If we want to find

$$w_1 w_2 (x) \quad \text{(sometimes written } w_{1o}\, w_2)$$

we take the function *nearest the x first*, in this case w_2.

For example,

$$w_1 w_2 (5) \; = \; w_1 \left[w_2(5) \right] \; = \; w_1 (-7) \; = \; 4 \times -7 \; = \; -28$$

but $\quad w_2 w_1 (5) \; = \; w_2 \left[w_1(5) \right] \; = \; w_2 (20) \; = \; 20 - 12 \; = \; 8$

If we compare this with $w(5) = 8$ we can see that it's the *second* of the two compositions that would be the same as the original function w.

We'll see why this is so by finding $w_1 w_2$ and $w_2 w_1$ as functions, but before we do this let's have a look at what the x actually means in a definition of a function. Really, it's a *dummy variable*, only there to show the effect of the function. It can sometimes be easier to understand what's happening if we replace the x by a box. Instead of:

$$f : \quad x \quad \longmapsto \quad \frac{x - 1}{2x + 1}$$

we could write:

$$f : \quad \square \quad \longmapsto \quad \frac{\square - 1}{2\square + 1}$$

and understand that the boxes have to be filled with the same quantity. So for example:

$$f : \quad x^2 \quad \longmapsto \quad \frac{x^2 - 1}{2x^2 + 1}$$

$$\text{i.e.} \quad x^2 \quad \longmapsto \quad \frac{x^2 - 1}{2x^2 + 1}$$

$$\text{and} \quad f : \quad x - 1 \longmapsto \quad \frac{(x - 1) - 1}{2(x - 1) + 1} \; = \; \frac{x - 2}{2x - 1}$$

$$\text{i.e.} \quad x - 1 \longmapsto \quad \frac{x - 2}{2x - 1}$$

Now let's go back to our two compositions $w_1 w_2$ and $w_2 w_1$ and see if we can write them as functions:

$$w_1 w_2 (x) \; = \; w_1 \left[w_2 (x) \right] = w_1 (x - 12) \; = \; 4(x - 12)$$

$$\text{i.e.} \quad w_1 w_2 : \quad x \quad \longmapsto \quad 4x - 48$$

Now for $w_2 w_1$

$$w_2 w_1 (x) = w_2 \big[w_1(x) \big] \quad = \quad w_2 (4x)$$
$$= \quad 4x - 12$$

i.e. $w_2 w_1 : x \; \mapsto \; 4x - 12$

and you can see that this is the same as w.

Let's have a look at another example of this.

Example	The functions f and g are defined by:

$$f: \quad x \quad \mapsto \quad 2x - 1$$

$$g: \quad x \quad \mapsto \quad x^2$$

Find fg and gf in a similar form and the value of x for which $fg(x) = gf(x)$

Solution	

$fg(x) \quad = f\big[g(x) \big] \quad = \quad f(x^2) \quad = \quad 2x^2 - 1$

$gf(x) \quad = g\big[f(x) \big] \quad = \quad g(2x-1) \quad = \quad (2x-1)^2$

i.e.   fg : $x \mapsto 2x^2 - 1$ and gf : $x \mapsto (2x-1)^2$

If $fg(x) \quad = \quad gf(x),$

then $2x^2 - 1 \; = \; (2x-1)^2 \; = \; 4x^2 - 4x + 1$

$$2x^2 - 4x + 2 \quad = \quad 0$$
$$x^2 - 2x + 1 \quad = \quad 0$$
$$(x-1)^2 \quad = \quad 0$$
$$x = 1$$

You have to be a little bit careful when combining two functions that have the form of fractions – suppose f and g are defined by:

$$f: \quad x \quad \mapsto \quad \frac{x-1}{x+2}, \quad x \neq -2$$

$$g: \quad x \quad \mapsto \quad \frac{1-2x}{1-x}, \quad x \neq 1$$

Then $fg(x) \quad = \quad f[g(x)] \quad = \quad f\left[\dfrac{1-2x}{1-x} \right]$

$$= \quad \frac{\dfrac{1-2x}{1-x} - 1}{\dfrac{1-2x}{1-x} + 2}$$

(At this point, to get rid of the $(1 - x)$'s on the bottom of the two fractions we multiply *everything*, i.e. all four terms, by $(1 - x)$. Leave the $(1 - x)$ in the bracket for the moment to avoid confusion with signs.)

$$= \frac{(1-2x) - 1(1-x)}{(1-2x) + 2(1-x)} = \frac{1 - 2x - 1 + x}{1 - 2x + 2 - 2x}$$

$$= \frac{-x}{3 - 4x} = \frac{x}{4x - 3}$$

You can see that it wouldn't be too difficult to make a mistake. It's not a bad idea just to check quickly with a suitable value of x, e.g. $x = -1$

$$fg(-1) \quad = \quad f[g(-1)] \quad = \quad f\left(\frac{3}{2}\right) \quad = \quad \frac{\frac{1}{2}}{\frac{7}{2}} \quad = \quad \frac{1}{7}$$

and from above:

$$fg(-1) \quad = \quad \frac{-1}{4(-1)-3} \quad = \quad \frac{1}{7} \quad \text{which agrees.}$$

The two functions that are combined don't have to be different functions – it's quite common to have to calculate something like f^2, where:

$$f: \quad x \quad \mapsto \quad \frac{x-1}{x+2}, x \neq -2$$

$$f^2(x) \quad = \quad ff(x) \quad = \quad f[f(x)] \quad = \quad f\left(\frac{x-1}{x+2}\right)$$

$$= \frac{(x-1) - (x+2)}{(x-1) + 2(x+2)}$$

$$= \frac{-3}{3x+3} \quad = \quad \frac{-1}{x+1}$$

(Check with $x = 1$: both give $-\frac{1}{2}$)

You should now be able to answer Exercises on 7, 8, 9 and 10 on p. 29.

Odd and even functions

There are two kinds of functions that have an interesting property.

Even functions: If f is an even function, then:

$$f(x) \quad = \quad f(-x)$$

When plotted on a graph an even function is symmetrical about the vertical axis. Some examples of this type would be:

$$x^2 \text{ (because } (-x)^2 = (+x)^2 \text{)}, 1 - x^2, \sqrt{1 + x^2}, \frac{1}{x^4 + 1}, \text{ etc.}$$

Odd functions: If g is an odd function,

$$g(-x) = -g(x)$$

This type includes:

$$x, x^3 - x, \frac{1}{x}, \frac{x}{1+x^2}, \text{etc.}$$

(You may notice from the last example that if you have an odd function (x) divided by an even function ($1 + x^2$) the result is *odd*. The same applies if the two are *multiplied* together, so that $x(1 + x^2)$ is also odd.)

You should now be able to answer Exercise 11 on pp. 29–30.

Periodic functions

A function which has values that repeat at regular intervals is called *periodic*. The interval distance at which it repeats is called the period. The most commonly used periodic functions are the trigonometric functions, such as sine, cosine and tangent, which you will meet later.

There are a number of periodic functions that don't involve trigonometry. For example, if we allow $[x]$ to mean the greatest possible integer that is less than or equal to x, then the function

$$f(x) = x - [x]$$

is periodic, with a period of 1 as the diagram below shows.

Figure 2.5

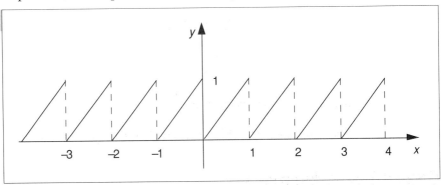

You might also like to note that this function has a restricted range $0 \le y < 1$ though the domain is unrestricted.

Graphs of functions

Even functions

You may already be familiar with the shape of the curve $y = x^2$.

Figure 2.6

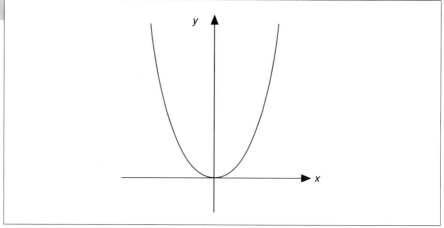

As you can see, the graph is symmetrical about the y-axis. This means that it's the graph of an even function. The graph of $y = -x^2$ is exactly the same but turned upside down.

Figure 2.7

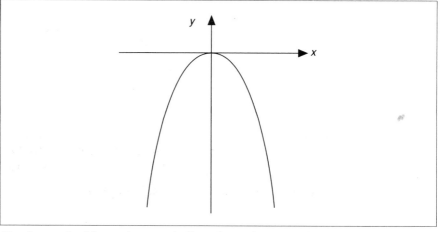

Further on in this section we shall see how changing the equation slightly has a corresponding effect on the graph. For the moment, let's have a look at the graph of another even function just to see its symmetry: you will not be expected at this stage to be able to work out the graph yourself (unless a you have a graphical calculator!).

Figure 2.8

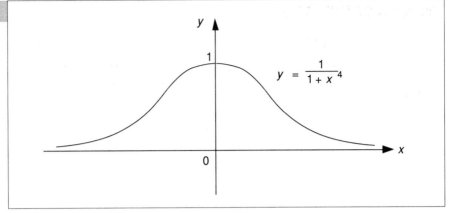

$$y = \frac{1}{1 + x^4}$$

Odd functions

The simplest odd function of all is $y = x$ and you will certainly be expected to be able to sketch this one!

Figure 2.9

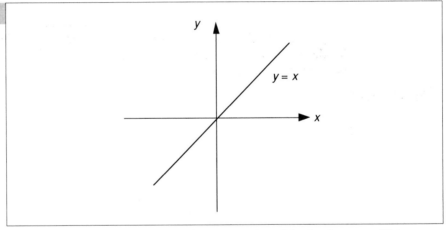

$y = x$

If you turn the page upside down, the graph still looks the same. This *rotational symmetry* is a property of odd functions. Two other common odd functions are $y = \frac{1}{x}$ and $y = x^3$. Their graphs are:

Figure 2.10

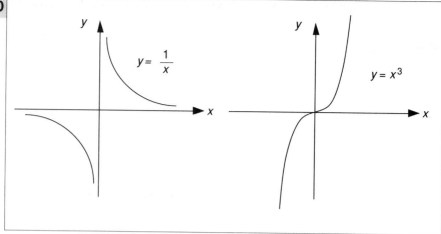

Inverse functions

Most importantly, we have to remember that a function only has an inverse when it's *one-to-one*: this means that the graph can have no turning points, like ∩ or ∪, anywhere. If you look at the graphs above, for example, you'll see that none of the even functions can have inverses, although an inverse exists for each of the odd functions.

> If an inverse exists, i.e. if a function f is one-one, then the graph of the inverse
>
> function f⁻¹ is a *reflection in the line y = x*.

Let's illustrate this with an imaginary curve which has been drawn so that there are no turning points:

Figure 2.11

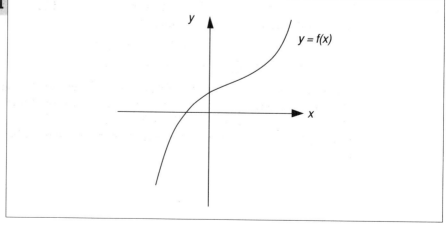

To find the graph of $f^{-1}(x)$, we draw in the line $y = x$ and reflect about this line.

Figure 2.12

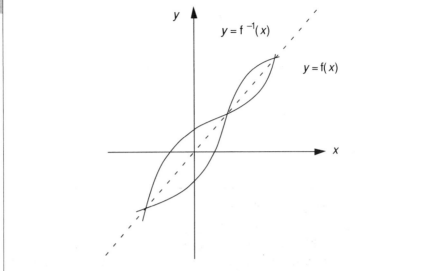

You should now be able to answer Exercise 12 on p. 30.

Transformations of graphs

We're going to see how the composition of functions can shift graphs around the axes and stretch or compress them, without making any major changes in their overall shape. We'll start with looking at the two functions:

$$f: x \mapsto x^2$$

$$g: x \mapsto x + 2$$

This is a classic example of how the order of composition of functions is important. Let's work out $fg(x)$ and $gf(x)$:

$$fg(x) = f[g(x)] = f(x + 2) = (x + 2)^2$$
$$gf(x) = g[f(x)] = g(x^2) = x^2 + 2$$

If we take the first of these two, $fg(x) = (x + 2)^2$, we can find some points and try and sketch the graph. For what value of x is the function zero? This will be when $x = -2$. When $x = 0$, $fg(0) = (0 + 2)^2 = 4$. Then we can see that since $fg(x)$ is the square of a function, it can never be negative. The graph looks like:

23

Figure 2.13

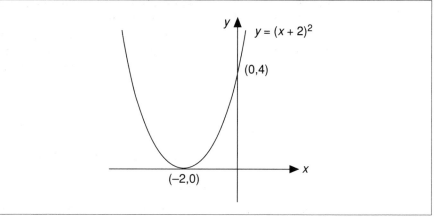

This is the same graph as $y = x^2$, with everything shifted two units to the left. We can write this as a general rule:

> The graph of $f(x + a)$ is the same as the graph of $f(x)$
> translated $-a$ in the x-direction.

Taking the second of the two compositions, $gf(x) = x^2 + 2$, and plotting the graph

Figure 2.14

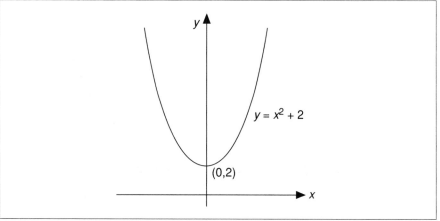

we find this is the same as the graph of $y = x^2$ shifted two units up. Again, there is a general rule:

> The graph of $f(x) + a$ is the same as the graph of $f(x)$
> translated a in the y-direction.

The effect of two further transformations is not so easy to see on the graphs that we have available: we have to wait until we look at trigonometric functions a little later on to appreciate them clearly. For the moment we will state the rules and apply them to some made-up graphs using straight lines. The two other transformations are represented by the functions $af(x)$ and $f(ax)$:

The graph of af(x) is the same as the graph of f(x)

with a scaling, factor a, in the *y*-direction

This means everything is stretched in the y-direction, with the corresponding x-coordinates unchanged. Suppose, for example, we had the function $f(x)$ with corresponding graph:

Figure 2.15

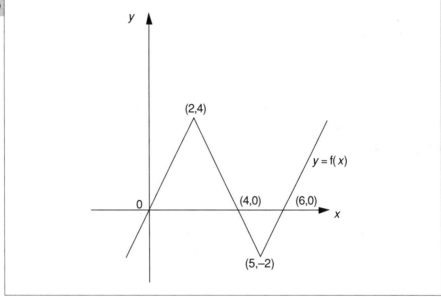

The graph of $y = 2f(x)$ would look like:

Figure 2.16

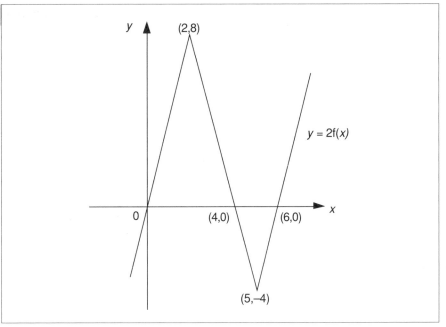

with all the *y*-coordinates doubled.

If *a* is a *negative* number, the graph is turned upside down, i.e. *reflected in the x-axis*:

Figure 2.17

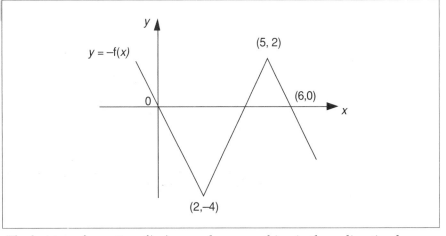

The last transformation, f(*ax*), squashes everything in the *x*-direction by *a*. More formally,

The graph f(*ax*) is the same as the graph of (*x*)
with a scaling, factor $\frac{1}{a}$, in the *x*-direction.

If we take $y = f(x)$ as in the previous transformation, figure 2.15, the graph of $y = f(2x)$ looks like:

Figure 2.18

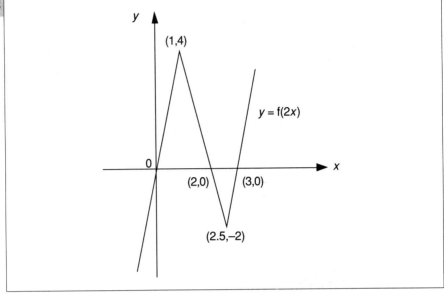

with all the x-coordinates halved while the y-coordinates are unchanged.

If a is a negative number, the graph is reflected in the y-axis. For example:

Figure 2.19

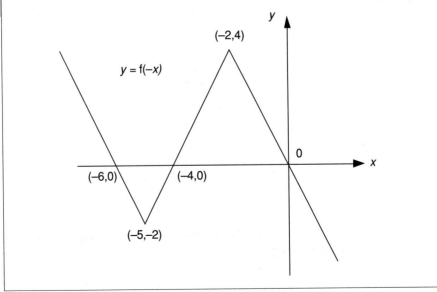

When we collect all these transformations together, we have the following table:

Table 2.1

Starting with the graph of y = f(x)

$y = f(x) + a$		translation a in y-direction
$y = f(x + a)$		translation $-a$ in x-direction
$y = af(x)$		scaling, factor a in y-direction
$y = f(ax)$		scaling, factor $\frac{1}{a}$ in x-direction
$y = -f(x)$		reflection x-axis
$y = f(-x)$		reflection y-axis
$y = f^{-1}(x)$		reflection $y = x$

You should now be able to answer Exercises 13 and 14 on p. 30.

EXERCISES

1 Find the value of g(2), g(5), g(0), g(–1), where g is the function:

$$g: \quad x \mapsto \quad x^2 + 2$$

2 Write the following rules as functions using first the transformation and then the equation notation.

    a   'multiply by 4 and add 3'   Call this 'p'

    b   'divide by 2 and subtract 2'   Call this 'q'

    c   'take the positive square root and double this.'   Call this 'r'

3 If p, q and r are the functions in [2] above, find p(2), p(–4), q(4), q(–8), r(100) and r(0).

4 Find the restrictions (if any) in the domain and range of the following functions.

    a   k: $\quad x \mapsto x + 1$

    b   l: $\quad x \mapsto \sqrt{x}$

    (remember that $\sqrt{\ }$ means the *positive* square root)

c s: $x \mapsto 2x^2 - 3$

d t: $x \mapsto \sqrt{x^2 + 1}$

5 For the functions we've introduced so far – p, q and r and k, l, s and t – state whether they are 1–1 or many to one.

6 Give the inverse of the following functions in a similar form, stating any restrictions on the domain.

a g: $x \mapsto 2x - 3$

b h: $x \mapsto x^3$

c k: $x \mapsto \dfrac{1}{1 + x}$; $x \neq -1$

d l: $x \mapsto \dfrac{2x - 1}{x - 3}$; $x \neq 3$

7 The functions f, g and h are defined by

f: $x \quad \mapsto \quad 2x$

g: $x \quad \mapsto \quad x + 2$

h: $x \quad \mapsto \quad \dfrac{1}{x}$; $x \neq 0$

Find f^{-1}, fg, gf, fh and gh. For what values of x does $f^{-1}(x) = fh(x)$?

8 Functions f and g are defined by

f: $x \quad \mapsto \quad 3x + 4$

g: $x \quad \mapsto \quad x^2 + 6.$

Using this notation, obtain expressions in the same form for fg and gf.

9 Functions f and g are defined by

f: $x \mapsto \dfrac{x - 1}{x + 2}$, $x \neq -2$

g: $x \mapsto \dfrac{1 - 2x}{1 - x}$, $x \neq 1$

Find gf(x)

10 Find g^2 where g is defined by:

g: $x \quad \mapsto \quad \dfrac{1 - 2x}{1 - x}$, $x \neq 1$

11 For the following functions, state whether they are odd, even or neither:

a $2x$ **b** $3x^2$ **c** $\dfrac{x}{1 + x}$ **d** $\dfrac{x^2}{x^2 - 1}$ **e** $\dfrac{x^2}{x^3 - 1}$ **f** $\sqrt{1 - x^4}$ **g** $x + x^2$

h $x^2 + 4x^4$ **i** $x^3(1-x^2)$ **j** $\dfrac{x^3}{x^2-1}$

12 Sketch the graphs of the following functions in their domains.

   a $y = \dfrac{x}{2}, 0 \le x \le 4$

   b $y = x^2 + 1, -1 \le x \le 2$

   c $y = x^2 + 1, 0 \le x \le 2$

   For each of the functions, state whether an inverse exists. If a function has an inverse, sketch the inverse on the same axes.

13 Sketch the graphs of the following functions:

   a $y = x^2 + 4$

   b $y = x^2 - 1$

   c $y = (x-1)^2$

   d $y = 1 - x^2$

14

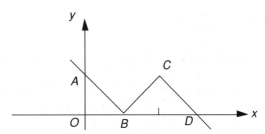

The graph of $y = f(x)$ is shown above. the points A, B, C and D have coordinates $(0, 1)$, $(1, 0)$, $(2, 1)$ and $(3, 0)$ respectively. Sketch, separately, the graphs of **a** $y = f(2x)$, **b** $y = f(x+3)$, stating, in each case, the coordinates of the points corresponding to A, B, C and D.

SUMMARY   In this section we have been concerned with formal definitions of relationships between variables, how these relationships can be expressed geometrically and how changes in the function affect the corresponding graph. You should make sure that you are familiar with these transformations as you will meet them again later on in your 'A' level work.

3

Rectangular cartesian coordinates

INTRODUCTION There are two commonly used ways of describing how the changes in one variable determine the changes in another. The first is to describe the relationship in algebraic form – an equation; the second is to describe it in geometric form – a graph. In this section we shall see how we relate a line on a graph to its corresponding equation and vice versa. We shall also introduce the modulus function and see the effect this has on a linear equation and its graph.

Rectangular cartesian coordinates

There are different ways of giving the position of a point in space. The most usual, and the one you're already familiar with, is to mark down a pair of axes at right-angles to each other and give the position of the point with respect to the axis. These are normally called the x- and y-axes and we say that a point is, for instance, two units along the x-axis and one unit along the y-axis, writing this in short as (2,1). These are called the *cartesian coordinates* of the point (after René Descartes, the French philosopher and mathematician).

Figure 3.1

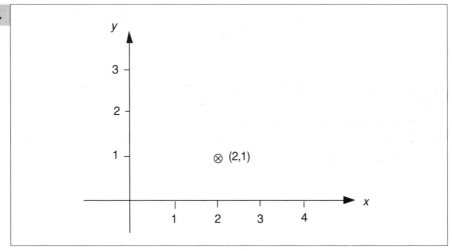

Suppose we plot another point on these same axes with co-ordinates (5,5), calling this point Q and the first point P.

Figure 3.2

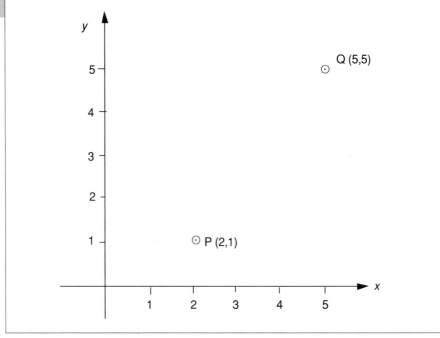

What would be the distance between these points? We find this by making a right-angled triangle with two of the sides parallel to the axes and calling the point where these intersect R.

Figure 3.3

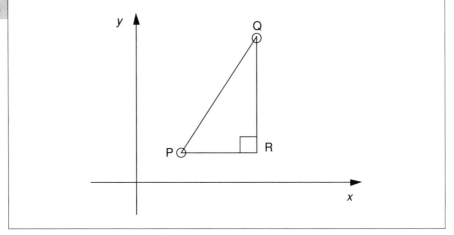

We want the distance PQ. The distance PR is just the difference between the x-coordinates, 5 – 2 = 3 units and the distance RQ is the difference between the y-coordinates, 5 – 1 = 4 units. Now we use Pythagoras' theorem:

$$
\begin{aligned}
PQ^2 &= PR^2 + RQ^2 \\
&= 3^2 + 4^2 \\
&= 9 + 16 \\
&= 25 \\
\Rightarrow \quad PQ &= \sqrt{25} = 5 \text{ units}
\end{aligned}
$$

This is true for any points,

$$\text{Distance}^2 = (x\text{-difference})^2 + (y\text{-difference})^2$$

and so if we call the two points (x_1, y_1) and (x_2, y_2) we have the formula:

> The distance between the points (x_1, y_1) and (x_2, y_2) is $\sqrt{(x_2 - x_1)^2 + (y_2 - y_1)^2}$

So for example, the distance between the points $(-3, 2)$ and $(4, -1)$ is

$$\sqrt{[4 - (-3)]^2 + [-1 - 2]^2}$$

$$= \quad \sqrt{7^2 + (-3)^2} \quad = \quad \sqrt{49 + 9} \quad = \quad \sqrt{58} \quad = 7.6 \text{ (1 decimal place)}$$

You should now be able to answer Exercise 1 on p. 40.

The gradient of a line

Equations involving only single powers of x and y, like $y = 3x - 2$ or $y + 2x + 8 = 0$, are called *linear equations* because their graphs are straight lines. If we plot some points for the first equation $y = 3x - 2$, say $(0, -2)$, $(1, 1)$ $(2, 4)$ and join them, we end up with the following line:

Figure 3.4

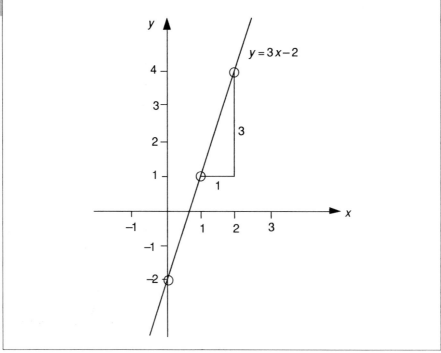

It is quite a steep line – as x increases from 1 to 2, y increases from 1 to 4. The ratio between y-increase and x-increase is called the *gradient*, so that

$$\text{gradient} = \frac{y\text{-increase}}{x\text{-increase}}$$

The gradient for the line is then $\dfrac{3}{1} = 3$.

As you may already know, we could have found the gradient of the line directly by looking at its equation and seeing the coefficient of the x-term. In the same way, by looking at the equation $y = -4x + 2$ we can say that it is a straight line with gradient –4. A negative gradient means that y *decreases* so much for every increase of 1 by x, so that the line slopes the other way.

Let's take two points from this equation, say $x = 0$, $y = 2$ and $x = 1$, $y = -2$, plot these and join them.

Figure 3.5

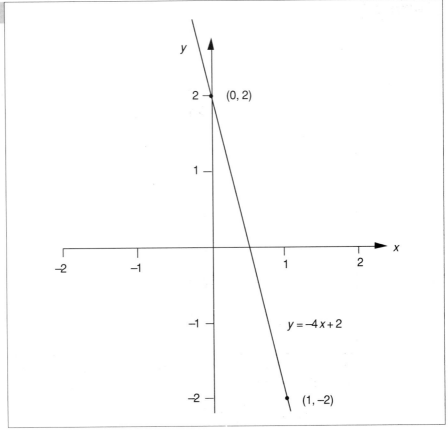

You can see that as x increases from 0 to 1, y decreases from 2 to -2, so that the gradient is $\dfrac{y\text{-increase}}{x\text{-increase}} = \dfrac{-4}{+1} = -4$, as we had already seen.

You should now be able to answer Exercise 2 on p. 40.

Parallel lines and intercepts

Lines with the same gradient are called *parallel*. If we take three parallel lines, each with a gradient of 3, say $y = 3x + 1$, $y = 3x - 2$ and $y = 3x - 5$ we can see that they cross the y-axis at different points found by putting $x = 0$ into the equations (since $x = 0$ on the y-axis), or simply by looking at the constant term after the x-term in the equation. This constant term is called the *intercept* and is usually written c when we need a general equation of a straight line.

Figure 3.6

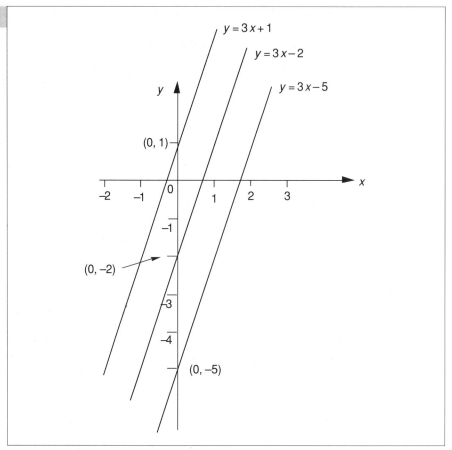

The equation of a line

The *general equation* is $y = mx + c$, where m is the gradient and c is the y-intercept. So, for example, a line with a gradient of 5 and a y-intercept of 4 has equation $y = 5x + 4$.

If we are told the gradient of the line and a point through which the line passes, we have to use a slightly different method to find the value of c. Suppose we are told that a line is parallel to the line $y = 3x - 2$ and it passes through the point (2,2). Since the line is parallel to the given line, it must have the same gradient, i.e. 3, so its equation is $y = 3x + c$ for some value of c. To find this value of c, we substitute the values of the x- and y-coordinates at the given point, which gives $2 = 3 \times 2 + c$ and solve this equation for c, i.e. $c = 2 - 6 = -4$. Putting this value of c back into our original equation, $y = 3x + c$, gives us the final equation:

$$y = 3x - 4$$

More frequently we are asked to find the equation of a line passing through two points: in this case, we find the gradient m from these two points and the constant c by substituting either one of the two points into the equation.

Example	Find the equation of the line passing through the points (2,3) and (5, –3).

Solution	The gradient $m = \dfrac{y_2 - y_1}{x_2 - x_1} = \dfrac{-3-3}{5-2} = \dfrac{-6}{3} = -2$

so we know the equation is $y = -2x + c$. Putting the first of these points into this equation, $3 = -2 \times 2 + c \Rightarrow 3 = -4 + c \Rightarrow c = 7$.

The required equation is $y = -2x + 7$ (or $y + 2x = 7$)

You should now be able to answer Exercises 3, 4, 5 and 6 on pp. 40–41.

The intersection of two lines

The equation of a line is not always written in the form $y = mx + c$: sometimes it can be written as $ax + by + c = 0$, for instance $2x - 4y - 3 = 0$. We shall look a little later on (in the section on simultaneous linear equations) at solving two equations written in this form, but for the moment we will suppose we have two lines written in the form $y = mx + c$ and we want to know where they intersect.

Suppose the two lines are $y = \dfrac{1}{2}x - 1$ and $y = -x + 5$. To find where they cross, we could sketch the lines and measure their point of intersection:

Figure 3.7

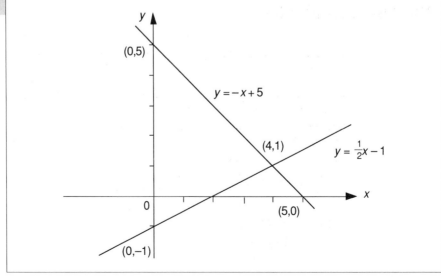

But generally, this method is too slow and anyway, unless the lines happen to cross at a point with convenient figures, as in this example, the result will not necessarily be as accurate as we would like. The algebraic method is to make the two expressions for y equal to each other, since the y-coordinates must be the same at the point where the lines cross.

$$-x + 5 = \frac{1}{2}x - 1$$

$$5 + 1 = \frac{1}{2}x + x$$

$$6 = \frac{3}{2}x \quad \Rightarrow \quad x = \frac{12}{3} = 4$$

Putting this back into either equation, $y = 1$, giving the point of intersection as (4, 1).

You should now be able to answer Exercise 7 on p. 41.

The modulus sign

The modulus of a function f(x), written $|\,f(x)\,|$, means that regardless of whether the value at any point is positive or negative, we always take the *positive* value. So if f(x) = 7, then $|\,f(x)\,|$ = 7; and if f(x) = –5, then $|\,f(x)\,|$ = 5. Let's compare the two functions:

$$g(x) = x - 2$$

and $\quad h(x) = |\,x - 2\,|$

For any value of $x \geq 2$, the value of the two functions are identical, e.g.:

$$
\begin{aligned}
g(7) &= 7 - 2 \\
&= 5 \\
\text{and} \quad h(7) &= |\,7 - 2\,| \\
&= |\,5\,| \\
&= 5 \\
\text{When} \quad x &= 2 \\
g(2) &= 2 - 2 \\
&= 0 \\
\text{and} \quad h(2) &= |\,2 - 2\,| \\
&= |\,0\,| \\
&= 0
\end{aligned}
$$

The difference begins as x takes values less than 2; when $x = 1$ we have:

$$
\begin{aligned}
g(1) &= 1 - 2 \\
&= -1 \\
\text{and} \quad h(1) &= |\,1 - 2\,| \\
&= |\,-1\,|
\end{aligned}
$$

$$= \quad 1$$

This is explained more clearly if we sketch these two functions in one graph:

Figure 3.8

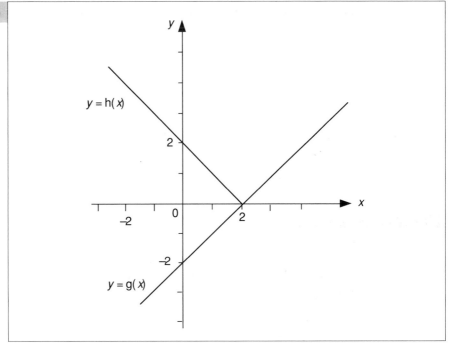

Sketching modulus functions

We shall be using the modulus sign further on in the course: you have to be able to sketch functions like $y = |x - 2|$ and $y = |2x + 3|$.

The important point in these graphs is to find out where the line meets the x-axis; since y cannot be negative, this represents the minimum value of the function. If we draw an axis through this minimum point, the graph is *symmetrical* about this axis:

Figure 3.9

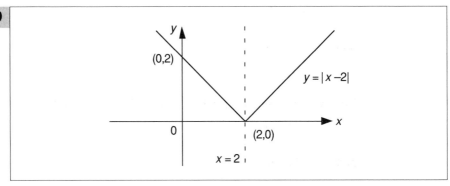

From the minimum point, we draw a line with the correct gradient on the right-hand side, in this case 1, and then reflect this in the line $x = 2$ for the left-hand side of the graph. Similarly for $y = |2x + 3|$, $y = 0$ when $2x + 3 = 0 \Rightarrow x = -\dfrac{3}{2}$ and the line on the right has a gradient of 2.

Figure 3.10

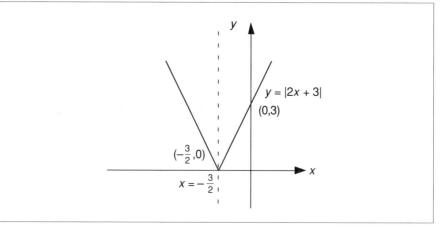

Actually, you can look on these graphs as being two halves of different lines: one line representing what the function is without the modulus sign and the other the same with *all* the signs reversed.

i.e. $y = |x - 1|$ is part of $y = x - 1$

         and part of $y = -x + 1$

         $y = |2x + 3|$ is part of $y = 2x + 3$

         and part of $y = -2x - 3$

We shall be looking at this later on.

You should now be able to answer Exercise 8 on p. 41.

EXERCISES

1 Find the distance between the following pairs of points:

   a   (2, 7) and (5, 3)

   b   (6, –2) and (1,10)

   c   (–3, –4) and (–9, 4)

2 For each of the pairs of points above, find the gradient of the line joining them.

3 State the gradients and intercepts of the following lines:

   a $y = 2x - 3$

   b $y = x + 4$

4 Find equations for the straight lines with:

    a   gradient 5, intercept –2

    b   gradient 1, intercept 0

    c   gradient –3, intercept 1

    d   gradient $-\dfrac{1}{2}$, intercept 2

5 Find the equation of the line which:

    a   has gradient 3 and passes through (3, 4).

    b   is parallel to the line $2y = x + 5$ and passes though (2, 4).

    c   passes through the origin and the point (2, 4)

    d   passes through (–1, 2) and (4, 5) ⋅

6 The straight line which passes through the points (6, 1) and (2, 3) crosses the y and x axes at A and B respectively. Find the area of the triangle AOB.

7 Find the points of intersection of the following pairs of lines:

    a $y = 3x + 1$ and $y = x + 3$

    b $y = x - 1$ and $y = -\dfrac{1}{2}x + 5$

8 Sketch the following functions:

    a $y = |x + 3|$ **b** $y = |3x + 1|$ **c** $y = |1 - 2x|$

SUMMARY

You will probably already have studied parts of this section, so perhaps you will not have found it too difficult. Make sure you're absolutely confident of being able to find the equation of a straight line from the various types of information you may be given, and that you can interpret the line equation quickly, together with a sketch of the corresponding graph.

4

Equations and inequalities

In this section we shall be looking at ways of solving different types of equations, occurring singly or in pairs. We shall also be looking at inequalities, where the solutions are not one single point but ranges of values.

Solving linear equations

This is the simplest type of equation and you are probably already familiar with it and quite skilful at its solution. The basic method is to expand any brackets first of all, and then collect all the xs on one side with all the constants on the other. We should then be able to find the solution by division.

Example	Solve the equations:

    a $3x - 1 \quad = \quad 2x + 4$

    b $3(x + 2) \quad = \quad 2(x - 1) - 5(x - 3)$

Solution   **a** $3x - 2x \quad = \quad 4 + 1$

                   $x \quad = \quad 5$

    b   Multiplying the brackets out,

        $3x + 6 = \quad 2x - 2 - 5x + 15$

$$\Rightarrow 3x - 2x + 5x = -2 + 15 - 6 \Rightarrow 6x = 7 \Rightarrow x = \frac{7}{6}$$

You should now be able to answer Exercise 1 on p. 54.

Simultaneous equations

There are times when we have a pair of equations with two unknowns, like $y = 2x - 3$ and $x + y = 9$, and we want to know what values of x and y we can find that make both equations true at the same time. In this case, we call them *simultaneous equations*. If we draw the graphs with these equations, the solution is the point (possibly more than one) where these lines or curves cross one another, as we saw in the section on intersection of lines. The solution for the pair of equations above is $x = 4$ and $y = 5$: we can see this geometrically if we plot both these lines:

Figure 4.1

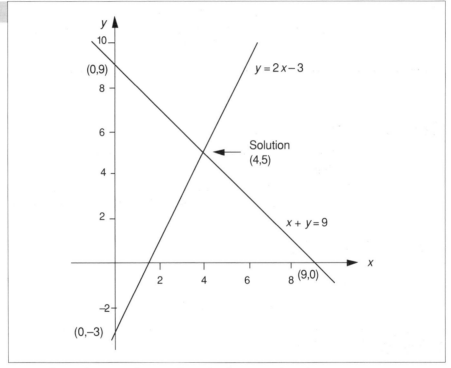

Apart from drawing the graphs, which we've already seen is quite time-consuming, we can use another method, the method of *substitution*.

Suppose for example we want to solve the equations $2y + x = 7$ and $5y - 4x = -2$. We make x the subject of the first equation by rearranging, $x = 7 - 2y$, and then substitute this expression into the second equation:

$$5y - 4(7 - 2y) = -2$$

In this way, we have eliminated x and we can proceed to solve the equation for y.

$$5y - 28 + 8y = -2$$
$$13y = 28 - 2 = 26$$
$$y = 2$$

We put this value back into the rearranged first equation,

$$x = 7 - 2y = 7 - 2 \times 2$$
$$= 3$$

So we have the simultaneous values $x = 3$ and $y = 2$.

To make the working easier, we try as far as possible to avoid fractions. In the previous example, for instance, it's probably easier to make x the subject of the first equation rather than y, which would have led to:

$2y = 7 - x \Rightarrow y = \dfrac{7 - x}{2}$, with slightly more complicated working.

Sometimes, however, using the method of substitution leads inevitably to fractions: the third method of solution avoids this problem, using multiplication rather than division. The idea is to multiply the two separate equations by suitable numbers so that we end up with the same coefficient in one of the variables. For example, suppose we started with the two equations:

$$2x + 3y = 13 \qquad\qquad [1]$$
$$3x - 4y = -6 \qquad\qquad [2]$$

If we multiply the top equation by 4 and the bottom by 3, the y-coefficient in both cases would be 12 (forgetting the sign for the moment):

$$[1] \times 4 \quad \Rightarrow 8x + 12y = 52 \quad [3]$$
$$[2] \times 3 \quad \Rightarrow 9x - 12y = -18 \quad [4]$$

When we add these equations (since the y-coefficients have opposite signs) we *eliminate the ys*:

$$17x = 34$$
$$\Rightarrow \quad x = 2$$

Putting this back into [1], $\qquad 4 + 3y = 13$

$$3y = 9$$
$$y = 3$$

So the solution is $x = 2$, $y = 3$.

We could instead have chosen to multiply the top equation by 3 and the bottom by 2 to give:

$$6x + 9y = 39 \qquad [3]$$
$$\underline{} 6x + 8y = +12 \qquad [4]$$

This time we have to *subtract* the equations in order to eliminate the xs, it's easy to make mistakes here. A safe method is to rewrite the bottom equation, changing all the signs:

$$6x + 9y = 39 \qquad [3]$$

[4] × –1   –6x + 8y = 12   [4]

Then we can add as before, to give:

17y = 51   ⇒ y = 3 and x = 2

You should now be able to answer Exercises 2 and 3 on p. 54.

Solving quadratic equations

We saw in the section on polynomials how we can factorise certain quadratics. If the equation we have to solve is in the form $f(x) = 0$ and $f(x)$ is a quadratic function which factorises, the solution is quite straightforward. Since the factors are multiplied together and the product is zero, one of them must be zero. From this we can find the two values of x which satisfy the equation.

Example	Solve the equation: $x^2 - 2x - 8 = 0$

Solution	Factorise first of all, $(x - 4)(x + 2) = 0$

Then either $x - 4 = 0$ ⇒ $x = 4$

or $x + 2 = 0$ ⇒ $x = -2$

Unfortunately, this method does not always work, because not all quadratics will factorise nicely with whole numbers. If we have already put a quadratic function into the completed square form we can sometimes solve related equations quite quickly. Suppose, for example, we had to answer the following question:

Example	

Let $f(x) = x^2 + 6x + 7$

a   put $f(x)$ into completed square form

b   solve the equation $f(x) = 4$

Solution	

a $f(x)$ $=$ $x^2 + 6x + 7$

$=$ $(x + 3)^2 - 9 + 7$

$=$ $(x + 3)^2 - 2$

b   If $f(x) = 4$, then $(x + 3)^2 - 2 = 4$

⇒ $(x + 3)^2 = 6$

We are going to take the square root of both sides.

Remember the ±! This is one of the most common mistakes made by 'A' level students.

$$(x + 3)^2 = 6 \quad \Rightarrow x + 3 = \pm\sqrt{6}$$
$$\Rightarrow x = -3 \pm \sqrt{6}$$

so $\quad x = -3 + \sqrt{6} \quad$ or $\quad x = 3 - \sqrt{6}$

Unless the question asks for a certain number of decimal places or significant figures, we can leave the answers as they are. Note that for any quadratic equation, we expect *two* solutions.

You should now be able to answer Exercises 4 and 5 on p. 54.

The quadratic formula

In practice, the numbers occurring in a quadratic equation can be rather awkward and it would take quite a while to find the solution by first completing the square. To save us trouble, there is a formula which will work for any quadratic equation: we just have to put in the figures and out the other end come the two solutions. Even though we have this last resort, we should still be able to factorise and complete the square!

What follows is the way the formula is arrived at. Though interesting, you will not be expected to reproduce it: you will, on the other hand, be expected to know and use the final formula!

Suppose we have the general quadratic equation:

$$ax^2 + bx + c \quad = \quad 0$$

where a, b and c are numbers. If we divide both sides of the equation by a, so that the coefficient of x^2 is 1, we have:

$$x^2 + \frac{b}{a}x + \frac{c}{a} \quad = \quad 0 \quad \ldots\ldots \quad [1]$$

If we want to put the expression on the left into the alternative form, the bracket will have to be $\left(x + \dfrac{b}{2a}\right)^2$ which means that the constant is $\dfrac{c}{a} - \left(\dfrac{b}{2a}\right)^2$

$$x^2 + \frac{b}{a}x + \frac{c}{a} \quad = \quad \left(x + \frac{b}{2a}\right)^2 + \frac{c}{a} - \left(\frac{b}{2a}\right)^2$$

so $\quad \left(x + \dfrac{b}{2a}\right)^2 + \dfrac{c}{a} - \left(\dfrac{b}{2a}\right)^2 = \quad 0 \qquad$ from [1]

i.e. $\quad \left(x + \dfrac{b}{2a}\right)^2 \quad = \quad \left(\dfrac{b}{2a}\right)^2 - \dfrac{c}{a}$

$$= \frac{b^2}{4a^2} - \frac{c}{a}$$

$$= \frac{b^2 - 4ac}{4a^2}$$

Take square roots of both sides, and then

$$x + \frac{b}{2a} = \pm \sqrt{\frac{b^2 - 4ac}{4a^2}}$$

$$= \pm \frac{\sqrt{b^2 - 4ac}}{2a}$$

i.e.

$$x = \frac{-b}{2a} \pm \frac{\sqrt{b^2 - 4ac}}{2a}$$

$$= \frac{-b \pm \sqrt{b^2 - 4ac}}{2a}$$

This is very important and is emphasised below:

> The roots of the quadratic equation
>
> $$ax^2 + bx + c = 0$$
>
> are $x = \dfrac{-b \pm \sqrt{b^2 - 4\,ac}}{2a}$

You may have met this before – but anyway it means that you can now find the roots for *any* quadratic equation by putting the coefficients into this formula. Let's see how it works, for example with:

$$2x^2 - 5x - 9 = 0$$

Here $a = 2$, $b = -5$ and $c = -9$. (Be *very* careful of signs when using the formula.)

Substituting, $x = \dfrac{-(-5) \pm \sqrt{(-5)^2 - 4(2)\,(-9)}}{2(2)}$

$$= \frac{5 \pm \sqrt{25 + 72}}{4} = \frac{5 \pm \sqrt{97}}{4}$$

so $\quad x = \dfrac{5 + \sqrt{97}}{4} \quad$ or $\quad x = \dfrac{5 - \sqrt{97}}{4}$

i.e. $\quad x = 3{\cdot}71 \quad$ or $\quad x = -1{\cdot}21$

(correct to two decimal places)

You should now be able to answer Exercises 6 and 7 on p. 54.

Simultaneous linear and quadratic equations

We may be given a quadratic equation and a linear equation and asked to find their common solution (there will usually be two).We can use the method of substitution, i.e. we take one of the variables from the linear equation, make it the subject and substitute this into the quadratic equation. Let's have a look at one of these.

Example   Find values for s and t which satisfy the simultaneous equations:

$$5s + t = 17$$
$$5s^2 + t^2 = 49$$

Solution   We rearrange the top equation to give:

$$t = 17 - 5s$$

and substitute this into the lower equation. Now it's just a question of some accurate algebra, and care with the signs:

$$5s^2 + (17 - 5s)^2 = 49$$
$$5s^2 + 289 - 170s + 25s^2 = 49$$

Take everything to one side:

$$5s^2 + 289 - 170s + 25s^2 - 49 = 0$$

combining and rearranging:

$$30s^2 - 170s + 240 = 0$$

We can usually divide through by something or other, here by 10:

$$3s^2 - 17s + 24 = 0$$
$$(3s - 8)(s - 3) = 0$$

i.e. $s = \dfrac{8}{3}$ or $s = 3$

Putting this back into the rearranged top equation gives:

$$t = 17 - 5 \times \frac{8}{3} = \frac{11}{3} \text{ or } t = 17 - 5 \times 3 = 2$$

We have the two solutions:

$$(s = \frac{8}{3}, t = \frac{11}{3}) \text{ or } (s = 3, t = 2)$$

You should now be able to answer Exercise 8 on p. 54.

Inequalities

If somebody asked us to put the numbers 15, 2, 18, 13, 9 in ascending order, we would be able to write them correctly as 2, 9, 13, 15, 18 without much difficulty. To express this relationship mathematically, we would use the $<$ symbol and write:

$$2 < 9 < 13 < 15 < 18.$$

As you probably already know, $p < q$ means that p is less than q, and $p > q$ means that p is greater than q, so for example the statements $2 < 9$ and $18 > 15$ are true. This is quite straightforward when we're dealing with positive numbers (although here's a puzzle you might like to try which is not immediately obvious: which is larger, 2^{333} or 3^{222}? No calculators!). We can extend the relation to include negative numbers if we say that:

$$a < b \text{ if } a \text{ is to the left of } b \text{ on the real number line.}$$

Here's part of this line:

Using this definition, we can see that $5 > 3$ but $-5 < -3$. This slightly strange turnaround of the $>$ sign is a property of inequalities – we can put it more generally as:

> If $p > q$ then $-p < -q$

So if we multiply an inequality by something *negative*, we must remember to *reverse the inequality sign*, e.g. $1 < 4$ is true, but multiply both sides by -2 without altering the sign and you'd get $-2 < -8$, which, by applying our definition, we can see is not true. We should write:

$$-2 > -8$$

Calculations involving inequalities

If we start again with $1 < 4$, and add 2 to both sides, we get $3 < 6$, which is perfectly true. Subtracting 4 from both sides of this last inequality gives $-1 < 2$, which is again true. Multiplying any of these three inequalities by 2 gives $2 < 8$, $6 < 12$ and $-2 < 4$ respectively, all of which are correct. Finally, dividing $-2 < 4$ by 2 gives $-1 < 2$: true; but if we had divided by -2, we would have $1 < -2$: not true. Division, then, is the same as multiplication: by *positive* numbers, inequality sign *unchanged*; by *negative* numbers, the sign is *reversed*. Addition and subtraction always leave the signs unchanged.

Inequalities containing variables

We'll be using these properties as we move on to inequalities containing *variables*, where, for example, we have to find the set of values of x satisfying:

$$x^2 + 4x - 8 > 0$$

or $\quad \dfrac{x^2 - 1}{x + 2} > 3$

We can treat these more or less in the same way as equations, except that in solving them there won't be single values of x but whole ranges. For instance, taking the simple example:

$$x - 1 > 2 \qquad\qquad\qquad\qquad [1]$$

we can see that there are any number of values of x which make this inequality true e.g. $x = 5, 6, 6.5, 6.893$ etc, etc. In fact, if we add 1 to both sides of the inequality, we get $x > 3$ and this is the solution. *Any value of x which is real and more than 3 satisfies the given relation.*

The symbol $\geq$ means 'greater than or equal to' (and $\leq$ 'less than or equal to'). If the inequality [1] in the paragraph above had been $x - 1 \geq 2$, the solution would have been as before, except that x could also take the value of 3. If we want to be quite precise and emphasise that we mean $x > 3$ rather than $x \geq 3$, we say that x is *strictly greater* than 3.

You should now be able to answer Exercise 9 on p. 55.

Inequalities with quadratic functions

We have to be careful when we see an inequality like $x^2 < 4$ not to assume that the solution is simply $x < 2$. If we look at a graph of $y = x^2$, we can see more clearly why this is so:

Figure 4.2

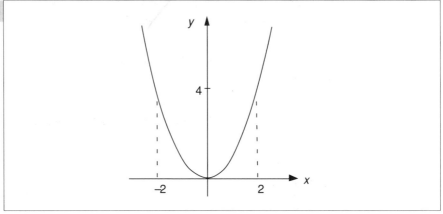

We want to find the values of x for which the corresponding value of y is less than 4, and we can see that the region $x < 2$ is only half the story. Since the square of a negative number is positive, any value of x less than –2, i.e.

more negative, makes $x^2 > 4$ which is not what is needed. So the only values of x which satisfy $x^2 < 4$ are those between -2 and 2, which we can write as $-2 < x < 2$.

The solution looks a little different for an inequality like $x^2 > 9$ because x can be in either of two regions, as we can see from looking at the graph of $y = x^2$ again:

Figure 4.3

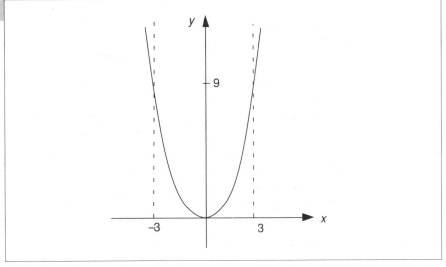

This time we want the value of y to be more than 9, which it is for $x > 3$ and also $x < -3$. Since these are two separate regions, we don't attempt to write them together. The solution is:

$$x < -3 \text{ or } x > 3$$

We use the same reasoning for slightly more complicated examples, remembering that there are two halves to think about. Suppose, for example, we had to solve the inequality:

$$(x + 3)^2 < 1$$

We 'take the square roots' of each side and then we have the two inequalities:

$$x + 3 < 1 \quad \text{and} \quad x + 3 > -1$$

These simplify to $x < -2$ and $x > -4$. This defines one region and we write the solution as:

$$-4 < x < -2$$

One more example:

$$(2x - 3)^2 > 9$$

This leads to the two inequalities:

$$2x - 3 > 3 \quad \text{and} \quad 2x - 3 < -3$$

Simplifying these, $2x > 6 \Rightarrow x > 3$

and $2x < 0 \Rightarrow x < 0$

These are two separate regions and the solution is:

$x < 0$ or $x > 3$

This method means that we can solve certain quadratic inequalities quite easily, particularly if we've already been asked to complete the square. Suppose we've found that $f(x) = x^2 + 6x + 10 = (x + 3)^2 + 1$ and we have to solve $f(x) < 3$.

Using the completed square form,

$$f(x) < 3 \Rightarrow (x + 3)^2 + 1 < 3$$

$$(x + 3)^2 < 2$$

$\therefore$ $x + 3 < \sqrt{2}$ and $x + 3 > -\sqrt{2}$

i.e. $x < \sqrt{2} - 3$ and $x > -\sqrt{2} - 3$

then the solution is $-\sqrt{2} - 3 < x < \sqrt{2} - 3$

Sometimes, particularly if we are given the function in factors, or we can quite easily put it into this form, it is quicker to use another method. Suppose we were asked to solve the inequality:

$x^2 - 5x + 6 < 0$ [2]

We start as we would with a quadratic equation – by factorising:

$(x - 2)(x - 3) < 0$

Now we have a product of two factors which is negative – so the factors must have opposite signs. The factor $(x - 2)$ is positive for any value of x more than 2 and $(x - 3)$ is positive for any value of x more than 3. Here's a diagram where the sign of the factors is shown in each of three regions:

Figure 4.4

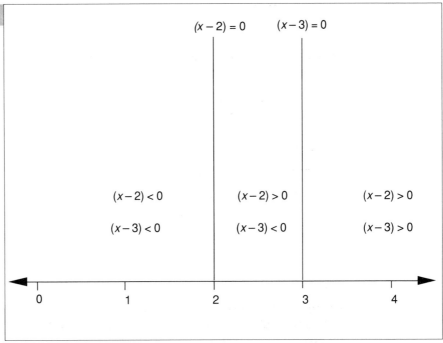

We can see from this that there is only one part of the number line where the factors have opposite signs – between the values of 2 and 3, when $(x-2)$ is positive and $(x-3)$ is negative. This is the solution, then: that x has to lie between these two values. Writing this as we did before, the required solution for [2] is:

$$2 < x < 3$$

Suppose the inequality sign in [2] had been reversed, so that we wanted to solve the inequality:

$$x^2 - 5x + 6 > 0 \qquad\qquad [3]$$

The diagram is exactly the same, except that now we're looking for parts of the line where the factors have the *same* sign. Now we want everything *except the part where* $2 < x < 3$, i.e. we want $x > 3$ or $x < 2$. Then the solution for [3] will be:

$$x < 2 \text{ or } x > 3$$

You should now be able to answer Exercise 10 on p. 55.

EXERCISES

1 Solve the equations:

   a $5x + (9x - 7) = 10x + 1$

   b $5(2x - 1) = 7(3x + 4)$

   c $4(2x - 9) - 3(x - 7) = 6x + 7$

2 Solve the following pairs of simultaneous equations by the method of substitution:

   a $y = x + 1$ and $3x + 2y = 17$

   b $3x - 2y = 5$ and $7x + y = 23$

3 Use the method of elimination to solve:

   a $5x - 3y = 1$ **b** $7x - 3y = 0$ **c** $4x - 5y = 7$
      $7x - 2y = 8$ $5x - 3y = 6$ $12x - 9y = 3$

4 Solve the following by factorisation:

   a $x^2 - 7x + 12 = 0$ **b** $x^2 - x - 12 = 0$ **c** $3x^2 + 10x - 8 = 0$

5 Solve the following by completing the square:

   a $x^2 - 2x - 35 = 0$ **b** $x^2 - 5x - 24 = 0$ **c** $2x^2 + 6x - 3 = 0$

6 Solve the following using the quadratic formula, giving your answers correct to two places of decimals:

   a $4x^2 + 7x - 1 = 0$ **b** $2x^2 = 9x - 5$ **c** $3x^2 + 8x = 2$

7 A power cable of length L metres hangs from two fixed supports at the same horizontal level x metres apart, and the middle of the cable sags by y metres.

It is known that $L = x + \dfrac{8y^2}{3x}$.

A cable of length 100 metres needs to be hung so that its sag is 10 metres. Calculate, correct to one decimal place, the required distance between its two fixed supports.

8 Solve the following pairs of simultaneous equations:

   a $x^2 + 3x + 5y = 20$

       $x + 3y = 1$

   b $2x + y = 8$

       $4x^2 + 3y^2 = 52$

   c $x + 2y = 5$

       $5x^2 + 4y^2 + 12x = 29$

9 Solve the following inequalities:

   a $x + 3 < 7$

   b $2x - 1 < 3x + 5$

10 Give solutions for the following inequalities:

   a $x^2 < 16$ **b** $x^2 \geq 5$ **c** $(x - 2)^2 < 9$ **d** $(3x + 1)^2 \geq 2$ **e** $x^2 - 3x - 10 < 0$

   f $x^2 + x - 12 > 0$ **g** $2x^2 - 5x > 3$ **h*** $x^2 - 6x > 1$

   *complete the square first

SUMMARY   Basic equations with exact solutions, which we've studied in this section, form an important part of this course and you should now be fairly confident of dealing competently with any one of the various types. Take particular care when squaring and multiplying more complicated expressions – for example, $(2x + 3)^2$ is not the same as $4x^2 + 9!$

5

Indices

INTRODUCTION   We're going to see in this section how a simple definition, $x^2 = x \times x$ can give rise to quite an elaborate topic in its own right. Various rules for manipulating these additional operations will be deduced and we shall finish with an introduction to the exponential function and its inverse, the logarithm.

Indices

You are probably quite familiar with terms like 5^2, 8^3 and x^4 already, and know that they stand for 5×5, $8 \times 8 \times 8$ and $x \times x \times x \times x$. These numbers, 2, 3 and 4, are called *indices* or *powers* and although small when written, have quite a dramatic effect on the size of the product. You might like to try working out on your calculator a few of them – but before you do so, try and estimate the approximate size of the answer: a thousand, a million, a million million? Have a guess and then work out the calculations:

a 2^{10}

b 4^8

c 12^6

d 6^{12}

How accurate were your estimations? I should think that unless you've had some experience in dealing with these powers of numbers, you almost certainly underestimated your answers – before you work them out, the figures tend to look deceptively small. While you've got your calculator by you, try a few more examples, this time with the idea of finding one of the rules for these indices:

$$2^4 = ? \qquad 2^6 = ? \quad 2^4 \times 2^6 = ? \quad 2^{10} = ?$$
$$5^3 = ? \qquad 5^5 = ? \quad 5^3 \times 5^5 = ? \quad 5^8 = ?$$

Can you see what these results are suggesting – and why it is? Writing out the first set without the shorthand, we can probably see this more clearly:

$$2^4 = 2 \times 2 \times 2 \times 2$$
$$2^6 = 2 \times 2 \times 2 \times 2 \times 2 \times 2$$

so $\qquad 2^4 \times 2^6 = 2 \times 2 \times 2 \times 2 \times 2 \times 2 \times 2 \times 2 \times 2 \times 2 = 2^{10}$

So for products with the same base number, we *add the powers*. Some more examples would be:

$$3^8 \times 3^{11} = 3^{19}$$

and $\qquad p^3 \times p^2 = p^5$

To see the importance of the numbers having the same base, try working out 2^5 and 3^4 and see if the product of these gives 6^9 – it shouldn't. This is quite a tempting mistake, try and avoid it if you can.

There is an extension of this result which can be a little confusing until you've had some practice. When there's a power of a power, something like:

$$(2^4)^3$$

it is tempting to add the two powers, as you would do if the expression was $2^4 \times 2^3$, but this would be wrong. In fact, $(2^4)^3$ is a short way of writing:

$$2^4 \times 2^4 \times 2^4$$

Now we *can* add these powers to give 2^{12}.

Try some more calculations:

$2^6 = ?$	$2^4 = ?$	$2^6 \div 2^4 = ?$	$2^2 = ?$
$5^7 = ?$	$5^3 = ?$	$5^7 \div 5^3 = ?$	$5^4 = ?$

Have you guessed what this is intended to show? Probably you have – to divide two numbers with the same base we *subtract the powers*, e.g.

$$3^9 \div 3^4 = 3^5$$

and $\qquad q^{10} \div q^7 = q^3$

As before, the base is important: $8^5 \div 4^3$ is *not* 2^2.

Zero as an index

This last property of subtracting powers creates some numbers that we haven't met before. If, for example, we divide 3^4 by 3^4,

$$3^4 \div 3^4 = 3^{4-4} = 3^0$$

and we have to give a value to 3^0. Logically this has to be 1, since we've divided something by itself. In fact we define *any* number to the power 0 to have the value of 1, as the 3 in the example could have been replaced without changing the result. This turns out to be quite consistent with both the rules we've found so far. If we look at an example using each of these:

$$4^5 \times 4^0 \quad = \quad 4^{5+0} = 4^5$$
$$4^5 \div 4^0 \quad = \quad 4^{5-0} = 4^5$$

we can see that multiplying and dividing by 4^0 leaves the result unchanged, which is what we would expect from something having the value of 1.

Negative indices

Another unfamiliar number appears when we apply the subtraction rule to something like:

$$5^3 \div 5^5$$

which gives 5^{-2}, a number with a *negative* index. If now we multiply this by the number with the corresponding *positive* index,

$$5^{-2} \times 5^2 \quad = \quad 5^{-2+2}$$
$$= \quad 5^0$$
$$= \quad 1$$

then divide both sides by 5^2, we get:

$$5^{-2} = \frac{1}{5^2}$$

So the negative power means *one over*, the *reciprocal*:

$$3^{-3} \quad = \quad \frac{1}{3^3} = \frac{1}{27}$$

$$2^{-2} \quad = \quad \frac{1}{2^2} = \frac{1}{4}$$

$$y^{-5} \quad = \quad \frac{1}{y^5}$$

If we have a look at a fraction where the negative power is already on the bottom, something like $\frac{1}{2^{-5}}$ for example, it works out as:

$$\frac{1}{2^{-5}} = \frac{1}{1/2^5} = 1 \div \frac{1}{2^5} = 1 \times \frac{2^5}{1} = 2^5 \ (= 32)$$

So we can see that negative powers take the corresponding term to the opposite position in a fraction, unchanged except that the negative sign is lost in the process.

You should now be able to answer Exercise 1 on p. 65.

Fractions as indices

Let's now widen the range of the indices still further and include *fractions*.

A simple example of this would be $9^{\frac{1}{2}}$. If we multiply this by itself,

$$9^{\frac{1}{2}} \times 9^{\frac{1}{2}} = 9^{\frac{1}{2} + \frac{1}{2}} = 9^1 = 9$$

we end up with 9. So $9^{\frac{1}{2}}$ must be the same as the square root of 9 (which can also be written $\sqrt{9}$, of course). Similarly, if we took $8^{\frac{1}{3}}$ and *cubed* this,

$$\left(8^{\frac{1}{3}}\right)^{3} \;=\; 8^{\frac{1}{3}} \times 8^{\frac{1}{3}} \times 8^{\frac{1}{3}} = 8^{\frac{1}{3}+\frac{1}{3}+\frac{1}{3}} = 8^{1} = 8$$

we end up with 8, so $8^{\frac{1}{3}}$ must be another way of writing the cube root of 8, i.e. $\sqrt[3]{8}$. When these fractions are fairly simple and the numbers are suitably chosen, as they were in the last two examples, we can find the value of expressions involving these powers without too much trouble. It helps to be familiar with the smaller powers of the first few numbers. We'll try a few of these. Note that if the top of the fraction is anything but 1, we deal with the *bottom* first.

Example Find the value of:

a $9^{\frac{1}{2}}$

b $8^{\frac{1}{3}}$

c $4^{-\frac{1}{2}}$

d $125^{\frac{2}{3}}$

e $49^{\frac{3}{2}}$

Solution a As we saw above, this is the square root of 9, so its value is 3.

b The cube root of 8 is 2.

c $\quad 4^{-\frac{1}{2}} \;=\; \dfrac{1}{4^{\frac{1}{2}}} \;=\; \dfrac{1}{\sqrt{4}} \;=\; \dfrac{1}{2}$

d $\quad 125^{\frac{2}{3}} \;=\; \left(125^{\frac{1}{3}}\right)^{2} \;=\; (5)^{2} \;=\; 25$

e $\quad 49^{\frac{3}{2}} \;=\; \left(49^{\frac{1}{2}}\right)^{3} \;=\; (7)^{3} \;=\; 343$

We know that the square root of a number, say 8, can be written either as $\sqrt{8}$ or $8^{\frac{1}{2}}$ and the cube root of 8 can be written either as $\sqrt[3]{8}$ or $8^{\frac{1}{3}}$ Similarly for higher roots – the seventh root of 8 can be written $\sqrt[7]{8}$ or $8^{\frac{1}{7}}$, for example.

This gives an alternative way of writing more complicated powers of numbers, e.g. $8^{\frac{4}{7}}$ can be rewritten $8^{\frac{4}{7}} = (8^4)^{\frac{1}{7}} = {}^7\sqrt{8^4}$. In general

$$a^{\frac{m}{n}} = {}^n\sqrt{a^m}$$

You should now be able to answer Exercise 2 on p. 66.

Surds

A surd is the square root of a positive real integer like $\sqrt{25}$ or $\sqrt{3}$. By definition, although in taking a square root we have two possible solutions, one positive and one negative, we take the positive square root, so that $\sqrt{4}$ means 2 and not –2. Since these numbers are *exact* as they stand, it's frequently preferable to keep them as they are and learn how to manipulate them rather than using a decimal approximation like $\sqrt{3} = 1.732$.

The rules for multiplying and dividing are quite simple:

$$\sqrt{x} \times \sqrt{y} = \sqrt{xy}$$

$$\frac{\sqrt{x}}{\sqrt{y}} = \sqrt{\frac{x}{y}}$$

So that, for example $\sqrt{3} \times \sqrt{5} = \sqrt{15}$ and $\sqrt{21} \div \sqrt{3} = \sqrt{\frac{21}{3}} = \sqrt{7}$. We can use the top rule to simplify the numbers inside the surd as far as possible,

e.g. $\quad \sqrt{50} \ = \ \sqrt{2 \times 25} \ = \ \sqrt{2} \times \sqrt{25} \ = \ 5\sqrt{2}$

and $\quad \sqrt{12} \ = \ \sqrt{4 \times 3} \ = \ \sqrt{4} \times \sqrt{3} \ = \ 2\sqrt{3}$

Rationalising the denominator

We prefer to have any surds in the numerator rather than the denominator if they occur in a fraction: the process of eliminating the surds on the bottom of a fraction is called 'rationalising the denominator'. In the simplest case, we have a single surd as denominator, something like:

$$\frac{6}{\sqrt{2}}$$

We than multiply top and bottom of the fraction by $\sqrt{2}$: by doing this, we square the denominator and clear it of surds:

$$\frac{6}{\sqrt{2}} \times \frac{\sqrt{2}}{\sqrt{2}} = \frac{6\sqrt{2}}{2} = 3\sqrt{2}$$

When the denominator consists of a mixture of numbers and surds, like $2 - \sqrt{3}$ or two different surds, like $\sqrt{5} + 2\sqrt{2}$, we use a different method which relies on the fact that $(a + b)(a - b) = a^2 - b^2$. So if we multiply either of the above expressions by the same expression with an opposite sign in the middle, we end up with the difference of two squares, which eliminates the surds:

$$(2 - \sqrt{3})(2 + \sqrt{3}) = 2^2 - (\sqrt{3})^2$$
$$= 4 - 3 = 1$$
$$(\sqrt{5} + 2\sqrt{2})(\sqrt{5} - 2\sqrt{2}) = (\sqrt{5})^2 - (2\sqrt{2})^2$$
$$= 5 - 8 = -3$$

Be careful when you're squaring mixtures of numbers and surds,

e.g. $(3\sqrt{2})^2 = 3\sqrt{2} \times 3\sqrt{2} = 9 \times 2 = 18$

Let's see how this method of multiplying by the opposite expression clears the denominator of surds.

Example

a Express $\dfrac{14}{3 - \sqrt{2}}$ in the form $a + b\sqrt{2}$

b Express $\dfrac{5}{2\sqrt{2} - \sqrt{7}}$ in the form $c\sqrt{2} + d\sqrt{7}$

Solution

a Multiply top and bottom of the fraction by the opposite of $3 - \sqrt{2}$,

i.e. $3 + \sqrt{2}$

$$\frac{14}{3 - \sqrt{2}} \times \frac{3 + \sqrt{2}}{3 + \sqrt{2}} = \frac{14(3 + \sqrt{2})}{3^2 - \sqrt{2}^2} = \frac{14(3 + \sqrt{2})}{9 - 2}$$

$$= \frac{14(3 + \sqrt{2})}{7} = 2(3 + \sqrt{2})$$

$$= 6 + 2\sqrt{2}$$

b This time, top and bottom by $2\sqrt{2} + \sqrt{7}$

$$\frac{5}{2\sqrt{2} - \sqrt{7}} \times \frac{2\sqrt{2} + \sqrt{7}}{2\sqrt{2} + \sqrt{7}} = \frac{5(2\sqrt{2} + \sqrt{7})}{(2\sqrt{2})^2 - (\sqrt{7})^2} = \frac{5(2\sqrt{2} + \sqrt{7})}{8 - 7}$$

$$= 5(2\sqrt{2} + \sqrt{7}$$

$$= 10\sqrt{2} + 5\sqrt{7}$$

You should now be able to answer Exercises 3 and 4 on p. 66.

The exponential function

The exponential function, e^x, is a particular member of the family of functions of the form a^x where a is a constant. The number e has rather a complicated definition: it is

$$e = 1 + \frac{1}{1} + \frac{1}{2!} + \frac{1}{3!} + \frac{1}{4!} + \dots$$

where ! means the *factorial* function ($6! = 6 \times 5 \times 4 \times 3 \times 2 \times 1$ and $4! = 4 \times 3 \times 2 \times 1$, for example). This gives us a figure of e = 2.7182818 ... (find it on your calculator by calculating e^1), so we can think of it just as a constant with a value slightly less than π (which is 3.14 ...) It has some interesting properties which we shall be looking at later. For the moment, let's have a look at the method for finding the graph of the function $y = e^x$.

Sketching exponential curves

All the curves of functions which are defined by

$$f(x) = a^x \qquad : a \text{ is a constant}$$

have a similar shape and one point in common. Can you work out what this point must be? If you recollect from the properties of indices, all non-zero numbers to the power of zero have the value of 1, so each of these curves passes through the point (0, 1).

Let's calculate a few points for the cases where $a = 2$ and $a = 3$

Table 5.1

$a = 2$, i.e. $y = 2^x$:

X =	0	1	2	3	4	5	6	7	8
y =	1	2	4	8	16	32	64	128	256

$a = 3$, i.e. $y = 3^x$ (try using your calculator to find the missing values):

X =	0	1	2	3	4	4.5
y =			9			

When we're plotting these points, we'll have to make allowances for the rate at which the y-values increase by compressing the y-axis, otherwise only the first couple of values will appear on our graph. A reasonable compromise is to take ten units to 1 cm on the y-axis, and one unit to 1 cm on the x-axis. This creates some congestion for the smaller values, but we can get a reasonable idea of the shape of each curve:

Figure 5.1

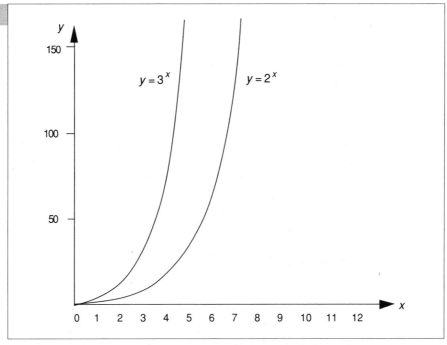

The graph of $y = e^x$, since e lies between the values of 2 and 3, lies between the graphs of $y = 2^x$ and $y = 3^x$. Since the numbers involved are not integers, we shall make a rough sketch of the function just to indicate its general shape:

Figure 5.2

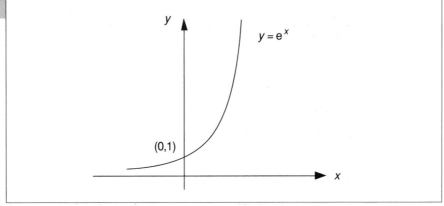

Note that all the transformations of graphs that we looked at in the functions section apply here, so that:

$y = e^{x+2}$ is the graph shifted back 2 units
$y = e^x + 2$ is the graph shifted up by 2
$y = e^{-x}$ is a reflection in the y-axis
$y = -e^x$ is a reflection in the x-axis

The logarithm function

If you look at the graph above, you will notice that there are no turning points: the function is one to one. This means that there is an *inverse function*, and this function is called the *logarithmic function*, written $\log_e x$ or $\ln x$. We shall be looking at these functions, logs for short, and their properties: for the moment, we are just interested in the shape of the graph. We'll draw the graph of $y = e^x$ and reflect this in the line $y = x$ for the graph of the inverse function, $y = \ln x$:

Figure 5.3

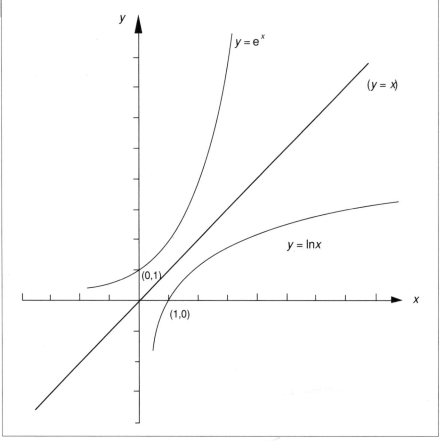

You can see that in both cases, the curve approaches more and more closely to one of the axes: e^x to the x-axis (negative) and $\ln x$ to the y-axis (negative). The curves never cross these axes (there is no real value of x

which makes e^x negative) and they are called *asymptotes*. If you are considering a transformation of one of the graphs, you must remember to take this into account: for example, $y = e^x + 2$ moves the graph up two units, so that the new asymptote is at $y = 2$ instead of $y = 0$ and it crosses the y-axis at $(0,3)$ instead of $(0,1)$:

Figure 5.4

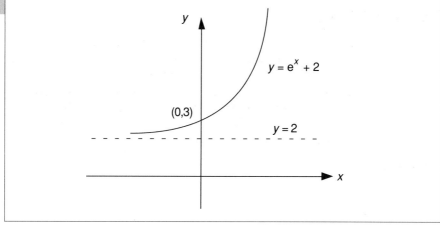

And $y = \ln(x - 2)$ moves the ln graph two units forward so that the new asymptote is $x = 2$ and crossing at $x = 3$:

Figure 5.5

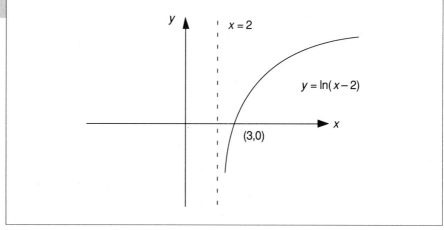

You should now be able to answer Exercises 5 and 6 on p. 66.

EXERCISES

1 Evaluate or simplify the following – try to do so without the use of calculators.

a 8^0 **b** x^0 **c** 2^{-1} **d** 3^{-2} **e** 10^{-3} **f** $\dfrac{1}{4^{-1}}$ **g** $\dfrac{1}{2^{-3}}$

h $\dfrac{2^2}{2^{-3}}$ **i** $\dfrac{3^{-3}}{3^{-4}}$ **j** $\dfrac{x^{-3}}{x^2}$

2 Find the value of:

a $25^{\frac{1}{2}}$ **b** $64^{\frac{1}{3}}$ **c** $8^{-\frac{1}{3}}$ **d** $27^{\frac{2}{3}}$ **e** $4^{\frac{5}{2}}$ **f** $\sqrt[3]{8^2}$ **g** $\sqrt[4]{16^3}$

Again, try to do these without the use of a calculator.

3 Express in the form $a\sqrt{b}$, where b is the smallest possible integer:

a $\sqrt{300}$ **b** $\sqrt{75}$ **c** $\sqrt{32}$ **d** $\sqrt{8}$ **e** $\sqrt{98}$ **f** $\sqrt{48}$

4 Express in a form clear of surds in the denominator:

a $\dfrac{10}{\sqrt{5}}$ **b** $\dfrac{21}{\sqrt{7}}$ **c** $\dfrac{5}{3+2\sqrt{2}}$ **d** $\dfrac{8}{\sqrt{14}-2\sqrt{3}}$

5 Sketch the graph of $y = e^x$.

Deduce the graphs of **a** $y = e^{x-1}$

b $y = 2 - e^x$

6 Sketch the graph of $y = \ln x$.

Deduce the graphs of **a** $y = 2 + \ln x$

b $y = -\ln(x - 3)$

SUMMARY We need to be fairly careful when working with indices: it's easy to make mistakes. Make sure you understand the basic rules, particularly the difference between $a^m \times a^n = a^{m+n}$ and $(a^m)^n = a^{mn}$ and the fact that a negative power means 'one over', so that $2\,a^{-n} = \dfrac{2}{a^n}$.

6

Sequences and series

INTRODUCTION When we study mathematics we frequently find ourselves searching for a pattern which relates different items of a collection to each other. In this section we shall be concerned with sequences and series of numbers – finding the pattern behind them and using this to find concise ways of describing them. There will be an introduction to the symbol Σ for the sum of a series, a useful device which you will meet again further on in the course. We shall then look at two standard types of series – arithmetic and geometric, devising and using general formulae by which we can find terms and sums.

Sequences

If we look at the sequences of numbers:

    2, 3, 5, 8, 12

there are two different problems we could be asked to solve. One of these is to find the next couple of terms, which is relatively easy. Another is to find the value of a particular term, say the hundredth. These two problems call for different methods of solution which come from two different ways of describing the sequence.

We'll start by looking at the first of these problems, to find the next two terms. If we take the difference between each pair of terms we find a pattern:

Table 6.1

Term	2		3		5		8		12
Difference		1		2		3		4	

and we guess that this pattern will continue so that the next two differences would be 5 and 6. This would make the next term $12 + 5 = 17$ and the next $17 + 6 = 23$.

It's useful when we're trying to investigate sequences to have some standard way of referring to the terms, so conventionally we write the first term as u_1, the second as u_2, the third as u_3 and so on. In the sequence above,

$$u_1 = 2 \quad u_2 = 3 \quad u_3 = 5 \quad u_4 = 8 \quad u_5 = 12$$

Then we found that:

$$u_2 - u_1 = 1$$
$$u_3 - u_2 = 2$$
$$u_4 - u_3 = 3$$
$$u_5 - u_4 = 4$$

and continuing this pattern, we could put:

$$u_{n+1} - u_n = n$$

where n stands for any of the numbers 1, 2, 3, …. We can rearrange this to give the formula:

$$u_{n+1} = u_n + n$$

This is called the *recurrence relation*: if we know the value of a particular term, we could work out the term above or below and continuing in this way we could work out any term in the sequence. To do this, however, we have to know a particular term, and usually we are given the first. For example, in the sequence we've been looking at the first term is 2, and the sequence could be defined by:

$$u_{n+1} = u_n + n \; ; \; u_1 = 2$$

If the first term is different, the whole sequence can be different,

e.g. if $u_1 = 1$, $u_2 = u_1 + 1 = 2$

$$u_3 = u_2 + 2 = 4$$

$$u_4 = u_3 + 3 = 7, \text{ etc.}$$

The general term

The second problem, that of finding the value of the hundredth term, is more difficult. It involves finding a formula that tells us the value of any particular term we choose. In this case, the formula has been worked out: it is:

$$u_n = \frac{1}{2}(n^2 - n + 4)$$

You can check that this gives us the correct value for u_1 (= 2), u_2 (= 3) … etc. It also tells us that $u_{100} = 4952$. In general, though, finding this formula, usually from the *recurrence relation*, is beyond what we need at this stage and we wouldn't expect any complicated examples. There are some straightforward cases we could have a look at where we can find the formula without too much trouble. Suppose we have the sequence:

$$2, 4, 6, 8, 10$$

where $u_1 = 2$ $u_2 = 4$ $u_3 = 6$ etc.: we can see quite easily that $u_n = 2n$. Another example might be:

$$1, 4, 9, 16, \ldots$$

Here $u = 1, u_2 = 4, u_3 = 9, u_4 = 16$ and recognising the square we could put $u_n = n^2$.

You should now be able to answer Exercises 1 and 2 on p. 82.

Types of sequences

There are four types of sequence that we must learn to recognise: convergent, divergent, oscillating and periodic.

A *convergent* sequence is one in which the terms get closer and closer to a particular fixed number, called the *limit* of the sequence. If we look at the sequence defined by $u_n = \dfrac{1}{n}$, the first few terms are

$$\frac{1}{1}, \frac{1}{2}, \frac{1}{3}, \frac{1}{4}, \frac{1}{5}, \ldots$$

and you can see that the terms are getting (slightly) smaller each time. By the time we reach the thousandth term, the value is getting very close to zero. In fact, we can make the value as close as we wish to zero: hence a convergent sequence with a limit of zero. The terms do not have to approach the limit from the same direction: they can be alternately positive and negative, as in the sequence defined by $u_n = \left(-\dfrac{1}{2}\right)^n$ which starts

$-\dfrac{1}{2}, \dfrac{1}{4}, -\dfrac{1}{8}, \dfrac{1}{16}, \ldots$. Since we can make the terms as close to zero as we care, the sequence converges to the limit of zero. Also, the limit of a convergent sequence is not necessarily zero: the sequence defined by

$u_n = 2 - \dfrac{1}{2^n}$, for example, has a limit of 2, whilst the sequence defined by

$u_n = \dfrac{n}{n+1}$ has a limit of 1.

When the terms of a sequence become larger in a definite direction, i.e. either positive or negative, the sequence is called *divergent*. Both the following sequences are examples of this type:

$u_n = 3n$ with first few terms 3, 6, 9, 12, 15, ... and

$u_n = 2 - n^2$ with first few terms 1, –2, –7, –14, ...

The first of these diverges to positive infinity and the second to negative infinity.

When the sequence belongs to neither of these types, it is called *oscillating*. The sequences defined by $u_n = (-1)^n n$, which starts $-1, 2, -3, 4, -5, \ldots$

and $u_n = (-1)^n \left(\dfrac{n}{n+1} \right)$ which starts $-\dfrac{1}{2}, \dfrac{2}{3}, -\dfrac{3}{4}, \dfrac{4}{5}, \ldots$

are examples of this type. (The first is said to oscillate infinitely, since the terms are getting larger in magnitude, and the second oscillates finitely since all the terms lie within a finite range of values, i.e. $-1 < u_n < 1$).

A *periodic* sequence is one in which at some stage the terms start repeating themselves. A familiar example of this is the time in hours, 1, 2, 3, 4, 5, 6, 7, 8, 9, 10, 11, 12, 1, 2, ... and it starts all over again. Some fractions give a periodic sequence of digits when expressed as a decimal, for example

$$\frac{27}{37} = 0.7297297297297 \ldots$$

As you probably know, this is called a *recurring* decimal. By definition, since a periodic sequence can neither converge or diverge, it is also an oscillating sequence.

Sometimes if we're given a *recurrence relation*, the behaviour of the sequence can depend on the first term. Suppose, for example, that we're given the sequence

$$u_{n+1} = (u_n - 1)^2$$

If $u_1 = 2$, the next few terms are 1, 0, 1, 0, 1 etc, and this is obviously *oscillating* between 1 and 0. It is also periodic. If $u_1 = 3$, the next four terms are 4, 9, 64, 3969 with an obviously *divergent* sequence resulting.

You might like to try for yourself what happens when u_1 takes a value between 0 and 2. You can simplify the calculation involved if you leave the display from the last term on your calculator and work with this. Let's say, for example, that I start with 1.5:

$$1.5 \xrightarrow{-1=} 0.5 \xrightarrow{x^2} 0.25$$

$$0.25 \xrightarrow{-1=} -0.75 \xrightarrow{x^2} 0.5625$$

$$\xrightarrow{-1=} -0.4375 \xrightarrow{x^2} 0.19140625$$

$$\xrightarrow{-1=} \ldots \text{etc.}$$

You'll find the sequence settles down to a mixture of two distinct sequences, i.e. it is oscillating.

You should now be able to answer Exercises 3 and 4 on pp. 82–83.

Series

Expressions like:

$$1 + 3 + 5 + 7 + 9 \ldots \quad \text{and} \quad 4 + 2 + 1 + \frac{1}{2} + \frac{1}{4} + \ldots$$

are called *series*: they are sums of sequences. There are different types of series, depending on the relationship between successive pairs of terms.

In the first series, you can see that a fixed number, in this case 2, has been *added* to each term to get the next term. Series like these are *arithmetic*. When the terms are *multiplied* by a certain number to get the next term, as in the second series where each term has been multiplied by $\frac{1}{2}$, the series is *geometric*. We shall be looking at these more closely, but first of all we shall introduce a piece of mathematical shorthand, the Σ-notation.

Σ notation

Σ, pronounced 'sigma', is the Greek letter S, used to stand for *sum*. In order to write down the first series we looked at, i.e. $1 + 3 + 5 + 7 + 9$ with $u_1 = 1$, $u_2 = 3$ etc, we need the *general* term, in this case $u_r = 2r - 1$. Then we decide where we want to start, $r = 1$ and finish, $r = 5$, and write:

$$\sum_{r=1}^{5} (2r - 1)$$

In English this means 'put the first value of r into the general term, then the next, then the next and keep going until you reach the top limit. Then add all these terms together'.

The other examples would be:

$$\sum_{r=2}^{10} (r^2 + 1) = \underset{r=2}{5} + \underset{r=3}{10} + \underset{r=4}{17} + \ldots + \underset{r=10}{101}$$

and

$$\sum_{r=0}^{8} \frac{1}{2^r} = \underset{r=0}{\frac{1}{2^0}} + \underset{r=1}{\frac{1}{2}} + \underset{r=2}{\frac{1}{2^2}} + \ldots + \underset{r=8}{\frac{1}{2^8}}$$

We have to be careful if we want to find the number of terms – there's a tendency with something like $\sum_{r=2}^{10} (r^2 + 1)$ to say that the number of terms is simply the top limit minus the bottom limit, i.e. $10 - 2 = 8$. Actually, because both the top and bottom terms are included, there are in fact $8 + 1 = 9$ terms. Another example would be $\sum_{r=n}^{2n} r^2$: here the number of terms is $2n - n + 1 = n + 1$, and not n, as you might think.

You should now be able to answer Exercises 5, 6, and 7 on p. 83.

Arithmetic progressions

Let's write down some examples of the first of these two types of series, arithmetic progressions (APs for short). If we start with any number, say 5, and add a second number, say 3, and add the 3 again, and again, and again… we'd end up with a sequence of terms looking like this:

$$5, 8, 11, 14, 17, 20, \ldots$$

The first term doesn't have to be a whole number and the number that we're adding doesn't have to be positive. We could start, for example, with $3\frac{1}{4}$ and add -1 each time and then this would give:

$$3\tfrac{1}{4}, \ 2\tfrac{1}{4}, \ 1\tfrac{1}{4}, \ \tfrac{1}{4}, \ -\tfrac{3}{4}, \ -1\tfrac{3}{4}, \ldots$$

Here are some more examples of this type of progression:

a $1, 3, 5, 7, 9, \ldots$

b $3, 3.3, 3.6, 3.9, 4.2, \ldots$

c $p, \ p+q, \ p+2q, \ p+3q, \ p+4q, \ldots$

The fixed amount that is added to each term to give the next is called the *common difference* and is written d. When d is positive, the sequence is increasing; when it's negative, the terms decrease. The first term is usually written a, so any arithmetic progression can be written:

$$a, a + d, a + 2d, a + 3d, a + 4d, \ldots$$

with different values of a and d. (So that the series $5, 8, 11, 14, \ldots$ which we put together first of all has $a = 5$ and $d = 3$, the next has $a = 3\frac{1}{4}$ and $d = -1$.) Now the second term is $a + d$ and the fourth is $a + 3d$, so we can see that the number of ds lags one behind the number of the term, so that the term is $a + 3d$. If we write the nth term as u_n, then:

$$u_n = a + (n-1)\, d$$

Summing the series

Now we'll see what happens when we add the first n of these terms together. Writing this sum as S_n, we get:

$$S_n = a + (a + d) + (a + 2d) + (a + 3d) + \ldots + [a + (n-1)d] \quad [1]$$

If we write this sum the other way round, we have:

$$S_n = [a + (n-1)d] + [a + (n-2)d] + \ldots + [a + d] + a \quad [2]$$

We now add these two series by adding the first term of the first series with the first term of the second series, i.e. $a + [a\,(n-1)d] = 2a + (n-1)d$. Then the second terms of each, i.e. $[a + d] + [a + (n-2)d] = 2a + (n-1)d$, and continue in this way until we add the last term of each series, i.e. $[a + (n - 1)d] + a = 2a + (n - 1)d$. Each pair of terms has the same sum, i.e. $2a + (n - 1)d$ and since there are n pairs, they total $n[2a + (n - 1)d]$. We have added S_n to S_n so

$$2S_n = n[2a + (n - 1)d]$$

$$S_n = \frac{n}{2}[2a + (n - 1)d] \qquad [3]$$

This is one way of expressing the sum to n terms of an arithmetic series. If we look at the first and last terms of the series [1], a and $a + (n - 1)d$ respectively, we can see that if we added them together we would have the contents of the brackets in [3], i.e.

$$S_n = \frac{n}{2} \{\text{first term + last term}\}$$

and this can be a useful alternative way of expressing the sum. The box below contains the general properties we've found so far:

If u_n is the nth term of an AP,

$$u_n = a + (n - 1)d$$

If S_n is the sum of the first n terms of an AP,

$$S_n = \frac{n}{2} \{2a + (n - 1)d\}$$

$$= \frac{n}{2} \{\text{first term + last term}\}$$

Let's have a look at some examples of this:

Example   Write down the first five terms of the AP with $a = 3$ and $d = 2$. Find the tenth term and the sum of the first 20 terms.

Solution   The sequence will be:

$$3, 5, 7, 9, 11, \ldots$$

The tenth term, $u_{10} = a + (10 - 1)d$

$$= 3 + 9 \times 2 \qquad = \quad 21$$

For the sum, using $S_n = \frac{n}{2} \{2a + (n - 1)\, d\}$ with $n = 20$, $a = 3$ and $d = 2$

$$S_{20} = \frac{20}{2} \{2 \times 3 + 19 \times 2\}$$

$$= 10 \{6 + 38\} \qquad = \quad 440$$

Example	Find the twentieth term and the sum of the first 30 terms of the progression beginning with

$$10, 8, 6, 4, 2, \ldots$$

Solution	Here $a = 10$ and $d = -2$

The twentieth term, u_{20} $= a + 19d$

$$= \quad 10 + 19\,(-2) \quad = -28$$

The sum of the first 30 terms, $S_{30} = \quad \frac{30}{2}\{2a + 29d\}$

$$= \quad 15\,\{20 + (-58)\} \quad = -570$$

Example	Find the sum of the first 50 even integers.

Solution	The fiftieth even integer is 100 – the first is, of course, 2.

Using S_n $= \frac{n}{2}\{\text{first term} + \text{last term}\}$

$$S_{50} \quad = \quad \frac{50}{2}\{2 + 100\} \quad = 25\,(102) \quad = 2550$$

Instead of being asked to find the sum of a series which we are told is arithmetic, the question could be put in Σ-notation:

Example	$$\text{Find } \sum_{r=2}^{12} (3r + 1)$$

Solution	Whenever we're given a question like this, it's always a good idea to write out the first few terms of the series.

This would be $\quad 7 \quad + \quad 10 + \quad 13 \quad + \ldots + \quad 37$

$\qquad\qquad\qquad\qquad r{=}2 \qquad r{=}3 \qquad r{=}4 \qquad\qquad r{=}12$

We can now recognise it as an AP and treat it accordingly. The number of terms $n = 12 - 2 + 1 = 11$,

and then using $\quad S_n = \frac{n}{2}\{\text{first} + \text{last}\}$

the required sum is $\quad \frac{11}{2}\{7 + 37\} \quad = \quad \frac{11}{2}\{44\}$

$$= \quad 11 \times 22$$

$$= \quad 232$$

Here's a trickier example where we have to derive an expression for the nth term from an expression for the sum of the first n terms:

Example   The sum, S_n, of the first n terms of an arithmetic progression is given by $S_n = pn + qn^2$. Given also that $S_3 = 6$ and $S_5 = 11$,

a   find the values of p and q

b   deduce, or find otherwise, an expression for the nth term and the value of the common difference.

Solution   **a**   We're given that $S_3 = 6$, so putting $n = 3$ into the expression for S_n,

$$3p + 9q = 6$$

i.e. $p + 3q = 2$ [1]

Similarly, for $S_5 = 11$

$$5p + 25q = 11 \quad\quad [2]$$

Multiplying [1] by 5,

$$5p + 15q = 10 \quad\quad [3]$$

Subtracting [3] from [2],

$$10q = 1$$

i.e. $q = \frac{1}{10}$

From [1], $p = 2 - 3q = 2 - \frac{3}{10}$

$$= \frac{17}{10}$$

b   The nth term, u_n, added on to the sum of the first $(n-1)$ terms, S_{n-1}, gives the sum of the first n terms, S_n:

Figure 6.1

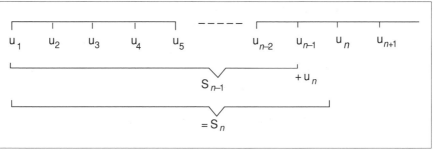

i.e. $S_{n-1} + u_n = S_n$

or $u_n = S_n - S_{n-1} = (pn + qn^2) - (p(n-1) + q(n-1)^2)$

$$= pn + qn^2 - pn + p - qn^2 + 2qn - q = p + q(2n - 1)$$

$$= \frac{17}{10} + \frac{1}{10}(2n - 1) = \frac{2n + 16}{10} = \frac{n + 8}{5}$$

This is the nth term, so:

$$u_{n+1} = \frac{(n + 1) + 8}{5}$$

The difference between u_{n+1} and u_n is the common difference d,

i.e. d $=$ $u_{n+1} - u_n$ $=$ $\dfrac{(n+1)+8}{5} - \dfrac{n+8}{5}$ $=$ $\dfrac{1}{5}$

You should now be able to answer Exercises 8, 9, 10 and 11 on pp. 83–84.

Geometric progressions

Remember that in a geometric progression (GP) we multiply any term by a fixed number (called the common ratio and written r) to give the next term. Some examples of this would be:

i)   1, 2, 4, 8, 16, ...

ii) $12, 3, \dfrac{3}{4}, \dfrac{3}{16}, \dfrac{3}{64}, ...$

iii) 5, –10, 20, –40, 80, ...

iv) $a, a^3, a^5, a^7, a^9, ...$

v)   1, 1.1, 1.21, 1.331, 1.4641, ...

From these you can see that r can be positive or negative, greater or less than 1. With the first term still written as a, sequence (i) has $a = 1$ and $r = 2$, and sequence (ii) has $a = 12$ and $r = \dfrac{1}{4}$. What are a and r for the remaining three sequences?

Our general progression can be written:

$$a, ar, ar^2, ar^3, ar^4, ...$$

and this time it's the power of r that lags one behind the number of the term (so that the fifth term is ar^4). The nth term is going to be:

u_n $=$ ar^{n-1}

Write out the sum of the first n terms:

S_n $=$ $a + ar + ar^2 + ar^3 + ... + ar^{n-1}$

$=$ $a(1 + r + r^2 + r^3 + ... + r^{n-1})$

Multiply both sides of this equation by $(1 - r)$:

$S_n(1-r)$ $=$ $a(1 + r + r^2 + r^3 + ... + r^{n-1})(1-r)$

$=$ $a[1 + r + r^2 + r^3 + ... + r^{n-1} - r - r^2 - r^3 - ... r^{n-1} - r^n]$

$=$ $a(1 - r^n)$

Then: S_n $=$ $\dfrac{a(1-r^n)}{1-r}$

This time there's no alternative way of writing the sum, although if $r > 1$ we can rewrite this as:

$$S_n = \frac{a(r^n - 1)}{r - 1}, \text{ so that the denominator is positive.}$$

Sums to infinity

Let's have a look at the series

$$1 + \frac{1}{2} + \frac{1}{4} + \frac{1}{8} + \frac{1}{16} + \frac{1}{32} + \dots$$

We can see quite easily that the sum of this series to

1 term,	S_1	=	1
2 terms,	S_2	=	$1\frac{1}{2}$
3 terms,	S_3	=	$1\frac{3}{4}$
4 terms,	S_4	=	$1\frac{7}{8}$
5 terms,	S_5	=	$1\frac{15}{16}$
6 terms,	S_6	=	$1\frac{31}{32}$

and so on, with the sum getting closer and closer to 2. If we use our formula for the sum to n terms, since $a = 1$ and $r = \frac{1}{2}$ here:

$$S_n = \frac{1\left(1 - \left(\frac{1}{2}\right)^n\right)}{1 - \frac{1}{2}} = \frac{1 - \left(\frac{1}{2}\right)^n}{\frac{1}{2}} = 2 - \left(\frac{1}{2}\right)^{n-1}$$

So the only difference between S_n and 2 is the term $\left(\frac{1}{2}\right)^{n-1}$; and as n gets very large, this term gets very small. We can make S_n as close as we like to 2 by choosing a suitably large value of n. In situations like this, we say that the *limit* of the sum of the series as n tends to infinity is 2, or in other words, the series *converges* with a limit of 2, and write:

$$S_\infty = 2 \qquad \text{(or S = 2)}$$

You can experiment yourself with your calculator, taking any number between –1 and 1 and raising it to a large power. No matter how close the number is to +1 or –1, if the power is large enough the result is very small. For example:

$$0.999999^{99999999} \approx 3 \times 10^{-44}$$

which, by most standards, would be considered small. This fact becomes significant when we look at geometric series whose common ratio r is between +1 and –1. Their sum to n terms, which we have seen is:

$$S_n = \frac{a(1 - r^n)}{1 - r}$$

simplifies as n becomes large. The second term in the bracket, $-r^n$, since r lies within the correct range of values, simply disappears, leaving the top line of $(a \times 1)$ or a, i.e.

$$S_\infty = \frac{a}{1-r}$$

(Putting $a = 1$, and $r = \frac{1}{2}$ gives S_∞ of the series $1 + \frac{1}{2} + \frac{1}{4} + \frac{1}{8} + \ldots$ the value of 2, which agrees with the value we found.)

Here are the results so far:

If u_n is the nth term of a GP,

$$u_n = ar^{n-1}$$

If S_n is the sum of the first n terms of a GP,

$$S_n = \frac{a(1-r^n)}{1-r}$$

If $-1 < r < 1$, this sum has a limit as n gets large, whose value is

$$S_\infty = \frac{a}{1-r}$$

We'll try applying these results to some examples.

Example For the following geometric progressions, write down the first five terms and find the general term and the sum of the first ten terms. If the series converges find the limit to which it does so.

a $a = 2,$ $r = 2$

b $a = -1,$ $r = -1$

c $a = 4,$ $r = \frac{1}{4}$

Solution **a** The progression is $2, 4, 8, 16, 32, \ldots$

The nth term, $u_n = ar^{n-1} = 2 \times 2^{n-1} = 2^n$

The sum of the first ten terms:

$$S_{10} = \frac{a(1-r^{10})}{1-r} = \frac{2(1-2^{10})}{1-2}$$

$$= 2(2^{10} - 1) = 2 \times 1023$$

$$= 2046$$

This series diverges as $r > 1$.

b The progression is $-1, +1, -1, +1, -1, \ldots$

The nth term, $u_n = ar^{n-1} = (-1) \times (-1)^{n-1} = (-1)^n$

$$S_{10} = \frac{(-1)(1-(-1)^{10})}{1-(-1)} = \frac{(-1)(1-1)}{1+1} = 0$$

There is no sum to infinity, because r has to be strictly greater than -1. (It is an oscillating sum, between -1 and 0.)

c   The progression is $4, 1, \frac{1}{4}, \frac{1}{16}, \frac{1}{64}, \ldots$

$$n^{\text{th}} \text{ term is } u_n = 4 \times (\tfrac{1}{4})^{n-1} = (\tfrac{1}{4})^{n-2}$$

$$S_{10} = \frac{4(1-(\tfrac{1}{4})^{10})}{1-\tfrac{1}{4}} = \frac{16}{3}\left(1-(\tfrac{1}{4})^{10}\right)$$

$$= 5.33332825\ldots$$

There is a sum to infinity since $-1 < r < 1$, and from our answer to S_{10} we can probably see what it is ...

$$S_{\infty} = \frac{a}{1-r} = \frac{4}{1-\tfrac{1}{4}} = \frac{4}{\tfrac{3}{4}} = \frac{16}{3} = 5.3333333\ldots$$

which is not a lot different from S_{10}.

Applications

These series do crop up in practical situations and we can use the techniques to calculate particular sums or terms in which we're interested. One such situation is investment at a fixed rate of interest – we'll have a look in some detail at an example of this.

Example   A 'Yearly Plan' is a National Savings scheme requiring 12 monthly payments of a fixed amount of money on the same date each month. All savings earn interest at a rate of $x\%$ per complete calendar month.

A saver decides to invest £20 per month in this scheme and makes no withdrawals during the year. Show that, after 12 complete calendar months, his first payment has increased in value to:

$$£20r^{12}, \text{ where } r = 1 + \frac{x}{100},$$

Show that the total value, after 12 complete calendar months, of all 12 payments is:

$$£\frac{20r\,(r^{12}-1)}{r-1}.$$

Hence calculate the total interest received during the 12 months when the monthly rate of interest is $\frac{1}{2}$ per cent.

Solution   After one month, the initial payment of £20 has a value of:

$$£20 + £20 \times \frac{x}{100} \quad = \quad £20\left(1 + \frac{x}{100}\right)$$

$$= \quad £20r$$

After a further month, this has increased to:

$$£20r + £20r \times \frac{x}{100} \quad = \quad £20r\left(1 + \frac{x}{100}\right)$$

$$= \quad £20r^2$$

This continues, so that at the end of each month the value at the beginning of the month is increased by a factor of $1 + \frac{x}{100}$, i.e. r. Since after the first month, the value is £20r and after the second, £20r^2, the value at the end of the twelve months will be £20r^{12}.

For the second payment, at the beginning of the second month, the value will be £20r at the end of the month, £20r^2 at the end of the next month, the third and so on. At the end of the twelfth month its value will be £20r^{11}.

Similarly for the payments in each succeeding month: each has one less month to earn interest and the value at the end of the 12 months decreases by a factor of r each time, i.e. the third payment will be worth £20r^{10}, the fourth £20r^9 and so on until the twelfth payment, having only had one month in which to earn interest, is only worth £20r.

The total of these value will be:

$$£\left[\, 20r^{12} + 20r^{11} + 20r^{10} + \ldots + 20r \,\right]$$

If we turn this round for easier working, this becomes:

$$£\left[\, 20r + 20r^2 + \ldots + 20r^{11} + 20r^{12} \,\right]$$

This is a GP of twelve terms with first term £20r. We use the formula $S_n = \dfrac{a(r^n - 1)}{r-1}$ since $r > 1$, and this gives:

$$£\,\frac{20r(r^n - 1)}{r-1} \quad \text{as required.} \qquad\qquad [1]$$

When the monthly interest rate is $\frac{1}{2}\%$, i.e. $x = \frac{1}{2}$,

$$r = 1 + \frac{x}{100} = 1.005$$

Putting this value into equation [1] with $n = 12$ gives:

$$£\,\frac{20 \times 1.005\,[1.005^{12} - 1]}{1.005 - 1} \quad = \quad £247.94$$

The total interest received will be the difference between this sum and the total of the payments, i.e.

$$£247.94 - 12 \times £20 = £7.94$$

You should now be able to answer Exercises 12, 13, 14, 15, 16 and 17 on p. 84.

Relationships between terms

For both kinds of progression that we've looked at, there's a common type of question which involves using the relationship between three successive terms to form an additional equation. If a, b, and c are three successive terms of an arithmetic progression, the relationship is:

$$b - a = c - b \quad (= d)$$

If a, b and c are three successive terms of a geometric progression,

$$\frac{b}{a} = \frac{c}{b} \quad (= r)$$

Let's have a look at these relationships in the two following examples:

Example   If $x + 1$, $x - 2$ and $\frac{1}{2}x$ are three successive terms of a geometric progression, calculate the possible values of x and the corresponding values of the common ratio.

Solution   We use the second of the relationships, i.e. $\dfrac{b}{a} = \dfrac{c}{b}$

Then
$$\frac{x - 2}{x + 1} = \frac{\frac{1}{2}x}{x - 2}$$

$$\begin{aligned}
(x - 2)^2 &= \tfrac{1}{2}x(x + 1) \\
x^2 - 4x + 4 &= \tfrac{1}{2}x^2 + \tfrac{1}{2}x \\
2x^2 - 8x + 8 &= x^2 + x \\
x^2 - 9x + 8 &= 0 \\
(x - 8)(x - 1) &= 0 \\
x = 8 \text{ or } x &= 1
\end{aligned}$$

$x = 8$ gives the progression 9, 6, 4 $\qquad$ where $r = \dfrac{2}{3}$

$x = 1$ gives the progression 2, -1, $\dfrac{1}{2}$ $\qquad$ where $r = -\dfrac{1}{2}$

Example	Find x if: $x, x + 5, 7x + 5$

are successive terms in an arithmetic progression.

Solution	Using the first of the relationships, i.e. $b - a = c - b$ to give

$$(x + 5) - (x) \quad = \quad (7x + 5) - (x + 5)$$
$$5 = 7x + 5 - x - 5 = 6x$$
$$\Rightarrow x = \frac{5}{6}$$

We can check this by substituting back

$$\frac{5}{6}, 5\frac{5}{6}, 10\frac{5}{6}$$

and we can see that there is a common difference of 5 between the pairs of terms.

You should now be able to answer Exercises 18, 19 and 20 on pp. 84–85.

EXERCISES

1 Give a recurrence relation for each of the following series:

  a $1, 4, 7, 10, \ldots$

  b $1, 2, 4, 8, 16, \ldots$

  c $2, 5, 10, 17, 26, \ldots$

2 Give the general term for the above sequences.

3 State whether the following sequences are periodic, oscillating, convergent or divergent.

  a $8, 4, 2, 8, 4, 2, 8, 4, 2, \ldots$

  b $2, 2\frac{1}{2}, 3, 3\frac{1}{2}, 4, 4\frac{1}{2}, \ldots$

  c $1, \frac{1}{2}, \frac{1}{3}, \frac{1}{4}, \frac{1}{5}, \frac{1}{6} \ldots$

  d $3, -9, 27, -81, 243, \ldots$

  e $1 + \frac{1}{2}, 1 - \frac{1}{4}, 1 + \frac{1}{8}, 1 - \frac{1}{16}, 1 + \frac{1}{32}, \ldots$

  f $1, -1, 1, -1, 1, \ldots$

4 Find the behaviour of the sequence defined by:

$$u_{n+1} = u_n^2 - 1 \qquad \text{when}$$

a $u_1 = 0$

b $u_1 = 2$

c $u_1 = \sqrt{2}$

d $u_1 = \sqrt{3}$

d $u_1 = -1$

5 Find the rule for each of these series and use this rule to say what the 10th term and the rth term of each series would be:

1		**2**		**3**	
Position	**Value**	**Position**	**Value**	**Position**	**Value**
1 →	3	1 →	3	1 →	1
2 →	5	2 →	6	2 →	5
3 →	7	3 →	9	3 →	9
4 →	9	4 →	12	4 →	13
5 →	11	5 →	15	5 →	17

6 Put the following series in Σ notation:

a $3 + 5 + 7 + \dots + 29 + 31$

b $3 + 6 + 9 + \dots + 96 + 99$

c $1 + 5 + 9 + \dots + 97 + 101$

7 Work out the first three and last two terms of the following series:

a $\displaystyle\sum_{r=1}^{15} (4r + 3)$

b $\displaystyle\sum_{r=0}^{10} (3 - 2r)$

c $\displaystyle\sum_{r=2}^{20} r^2$

8 Write out the first five terms and find the tenth term and sum of the first 16 terms of the arithmetic progressions where:

a $a = 3, \quad d = 1$

b $a = -2, \quad d = 3$

c $a = 100, \quad d = -4$

9 Find the twentieth term and sum of the first 20 terms of the sequences:

   a   1, 5, 9, 13, …

   b   2, 2.2, 2.4, 2.6, …

   c   240, 220, 200, 180, …

10 An arithmetic series is such that the sum of its first ten terms is 20, and the sum of its first 20 terms is 10. Find the sum of its first 40 terms.

11 The nth term of a progression is $np + q$ and the sum of n terms is denoted by S_n. Given that the sixth term is 4 times the second term and that $S_3 = 12$, find the value of p and of q.

12 Write out the first five terms, find the tenth term, the sum of the first ten terms and the sum to infinity of the geometric series with $a = 8$, $r = \dfrac{1}{2}$.

13 Evaluate to two significant figures:

$$\sum_{n=1}^{20}(1.1)^n$$

14 Find $\displaystyle\sum_{r=1}^{10} (r + 2^r)$

15 A man divides £1005 amongst four children, the amounts allocated being in geometric progression. Given that the largest amount is eight times the smallest amount, find the amounts allocated to each of the children.

16 In a car with four gears, the maximum speed in bottom gear is 20 kmh^{-1} and the maximum speed in top gear is 200 kmh^{-1}. Given that the maximum speeds in each gear form a geometric series, calculate, in kmh^{-1} to 1 decimal place, the maximum speeds in the two intermediate gears.

17 An employee started work for a new company on 1st January, 1992. Her salary for 1992 is £7000. The salary is revised each year, any increase becoming effective from 1st January. She estimates that each annual increment will be 8% of the previous year's salary.

   a   Write down her estimated salaries for the years 1993 and 1994.

   b   Write down an expression for £S, the *total* which she expects to have earned after n complete years, including 1992.

   c   Calculate, to the nearest 100, the value of S for $n = 10$.

18 Find the two values of x for which 1, x^2, x are successive terms of an arithmetic progression.

19 The first three terms of a geometric series are 1, x, y, and the first three terms of an arithmetic series are 1, x, $-y$. Prove that $x^2 + 2x - 1 = 0$, and hence find y given that x is positive.

20 A geometric series has first term 1 and common ratio r. Given that the sum of the first three terms is seven times the third term, find the two possible values of r.

Find the sum to infinity of each of the corresponding series.

SUMMARY

This has been quite a long section, with a good amount of new material. If you find you have problems with the Σ notation, it may help to write the first four terms, the resulting series then has a more familiar look to it and you will probably be able to proceed from there. When answering questions on arithmetic and geometric progression make sure you read the question carefully and distinguish between the nth term and the sum to n terms.

7

Trigonometry

INTRODUCTION We start this section by introducing a new measure for angles – the radian. Then we shall see how by extending our definitions of the sine, cosine and tangent functions we can find the value of these for any angle and derive their corresponding graphs. We will have a closer look at these graphs and their properties and also see what effect the transformations we studied earlier have on them. Finally, we shall see how we can use our knowledge of the functions to solve equations within a given range of values.

Radians

We usually measure angles in *degrees* – comparing the size of the angle with the 360° that make up a complete revolution.

Figure 7.1

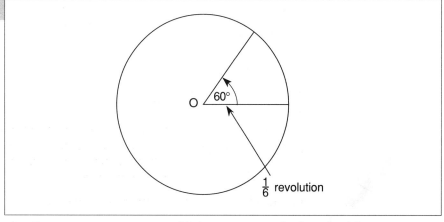

Another way we can express this is to compare the length of the arc subtending the angle with the perimeter of the whole circle. The unit used in this case is the **radian**, the angle at the centre when the length of the arc is the same as the radius of the circle.

Figure 7.2

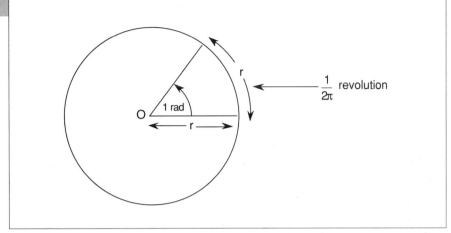

We write one radian as 1 rad, as you can see in Figure 7.2, or simply as 1 if we know we are dealing with radians. Since the perimeter of the circle is $2\pi r$, it will require 2π radians to complete the revolution, i.e.:

$$2\pi \text{ radians} = 360 \text{ degrees}$$

and $\quad$ 1 radian $\quad = \dfrac{360°}{2\pi}$

$$= 57 \cdot 29578\ldots°$$

This is not a very convenient number. In practice we express radians as fractions of π. With 2π radians equivalent to 360°, π radians = 180° and some other common angles are:

$$90° = \frac{\pi}{2} : 30° = \frac{\pi}{6} : 120° = \frac{2\pi}{3}$$

Working the other way round:

$$\frac{\pi}{4} = 45° : \frac{\pi}{10} = 18° : \frac{7\pi}{6} = 210°$$

You will need to use radians later on, especially in integration, curve-sketching and solving equations, when there are mixtures of algebraic and trigonometric functions. For the moment, it's important to get used to changing from one system to the other and recognising the common angles.

You should now be able to answer Exercises 1 and 2 on p. 103.

Arcs and areas of segments

The perimeter of a circle is $2\pi r$, and its area is πr^2. If we take a sector of a circle, its arc length and area will be a fraction of the whole – half a circle has an arc length of $\frac{1}{2} \times 2\pi r = \pi r$ units and an area of $\frac{1}{2} \times \pi r^2 = \frac{\pi r^2}{2}$ square units, for example.

We measure the fraction by the proportion of the central angle to 360° or 2π radians. An angle of 60° is then $\frac{60}{360} = \frac{1}{6}$ th of the whole, so a sector of radius 5 cm with a subtended angle of 60° has an arc length of $\frac{1}{6} \times 2\pi r = \frac{10\pi}{6} = \frac{5\pi}{3}$ cm and an area of $\frac{1}{6} \times \pi r^2 = \frac{25\pi^2}{6}$ cm².

Figure 7.3

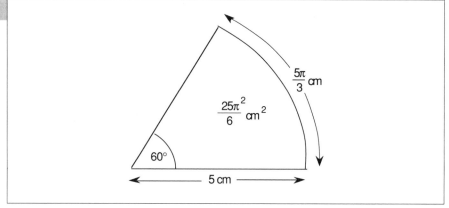

If the angle is given in radians, there is a neat formula by which we can find the arc length, and another for the area:

Figure 7.4

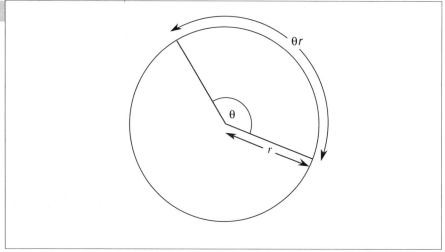

Suppose the subtended angle is θ radians, and the radius r: the arc length is:

$$S = \frac{\theta}{2\pi} \times 2\pi r = \theta r \qquad \text{[A]}$$

and the area is:

$$A = \frac{\theta}{2\pi} \times \pi r^2 = \frac{1}{2} \theta r^2 \qquad \text{[B]}$$

These are quite important, but luckily they are easy to work out for yourself if you forget them.

| **Example** | A sector of a circle has arc length of 30 cm. If the radius of the circle is 12 cm, find the area of the sector. |

Solution

Figure 7.5

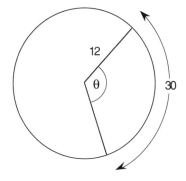

Using the formula for arc length above,

$$s = r\theta \Rightarrow 30 = 12\theta \Rightarrow \theta = \frac{30}{12} = \frac{5}{2} \text{ (radians)}$$

Using formula for area, $A = \frac{1}{2}r^2\theta = \frac{1}{2} \times 12^2 \times \frac{5}{2} = 180 \text{ cm}^2$

You should now be able to answer Exercise 3 on p. 104.

The sine of any angle

We're used to the idea that the sine of an angle is the ratio of the opposite side to the hypotenuse in a right-angled triangle. This definition can be extended to give a value for sine of any angle:

As a point P moves round a unit circle with centre the origin O,

the value of sin θ, where θ is the angle OP makes with the positive *x*-axis,

is the *y-coordinate* of the point P.

The advantage of this definition is that it covers all different cases when θ is between 0 and 90°:

Figure 7.6

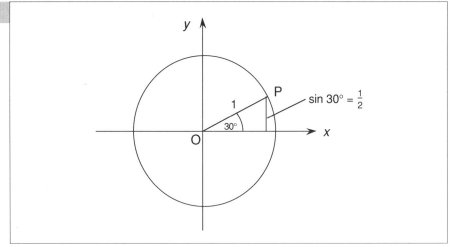

When θ is more than 90°, say at 210° (since P is below the *x*-axis, the *y*-coordinate of P, or sin θ in other words, is negative):

Figure 7.7

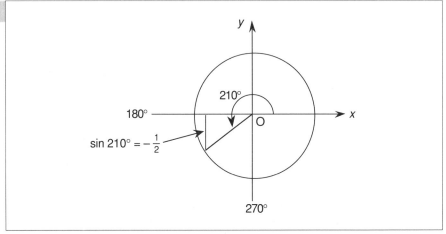

When θ is more than 360°, because when it reaches 360°, it starts again at zero, so that sin 390° is the same as sin 30°, i.e. $\frac{1}{2}$:

Figure 7.8

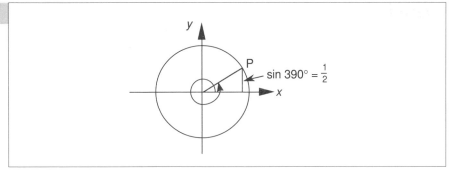

If we draw a new pair of axes and plot the angle θ along the *x*-axis and the *y*-coordinate of P along the *y*-axis, we get a curve which looks something like this ...

Figure 7.9

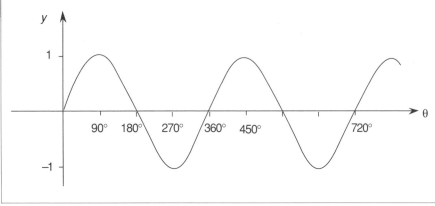

You can see that it passes through the origin, because when θ is zero, P is on the *x*-axis, i.e. $y = 0$.

It also has a maximum value of 1, and a minimum value of –1 when θ is 90° and 270° respectively, which is when P is right at the top and bottom of the circle. You can see that at 360° the whole graph starts again, repeating itself exactly. This is an example of a *periodic function* which was mentioned in the section on functions: the *period* in this case is 360° (or 2π in radians). It's also an example of a many-one function, since many *x*-values (i.e. from the domain) are mapped onto the same *y*-value (i.e. the range).

The cosine of any angle

Cos θ has a similar definition, except that this time as the point moves round the circle we take the value of the *x*-coordinate. This means that after P has reached the top, when θ is 90, cos θ becomes negative for a while since the *x*-coordinate of P is negative.

Figure 7.10

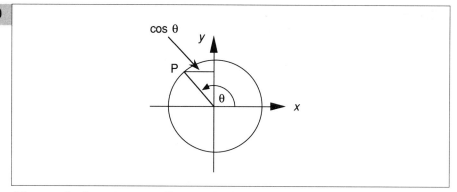

The graph of cos θ is actually exactly the same as sin θ except that it has been shifted back 90°.

Figure 7.11

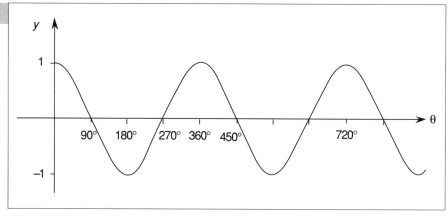

The maximum value is now when θ is 0°, and you can see that the graph is negative when θ is more than 90°, reaching a minimum at 180° until P is at the bottom of the circle at 270° where the *x*-coordinate is zero. It then increases until a new maximum of 1 when θ is 360° and so on, over and over again.

In fact, both the graph of sin θ and that of cos θ can be continued backwards if we allow the point to travel clockwise, which means the angle is decreasing. The graphs then look like this ...

Figure 7.12

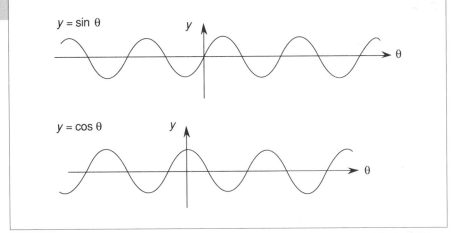

If you rotate the positive part of the graph of $y = \sin \theta$ by 180°, you would end up with the negative part. Sin θ is an *odd function*.

You can see quite an obvious symmetry for $y = \cos \theta$ around the y-axis. It is an *even function*.

The tangent of any angle

The final function we have to look at is that of tan θ. It is defined simply as:

$$\tan \theta = \frac{\sin \theta}{\cos \theta}$$

It doesn't look anything like either of the other two graphs, because of the cos θ as denominator. When cos θ is very small, which means that θ is close to 90°, tan θ becomes very large. Try and find the value of tan 89.99° and you'll see this for yourself.

When θ is actually 90°, the denominator of the fraction is zero and the value of tan θ is undefined (your calculator will just display E). To show this on the graph, we put in a dotted line (called an asymptote) at θ = 90°. Just after 90°, cos θ is still very small, but it's now *negative*. Since sin θ is still positive, tan θ will also be negative but extremely large. The graph jumps from the top of the page to the bottom – when the graph has a break like this, we say that the function is *discontinuous*. After 180°, both sin θ and cos θ are negative, so that tan θ becomes positive once more, building up to another asymptote when cos θ is zero again, which is at 270°.

Again, we can continue the graph backwards and we end up with something like this …

Figure 7.13

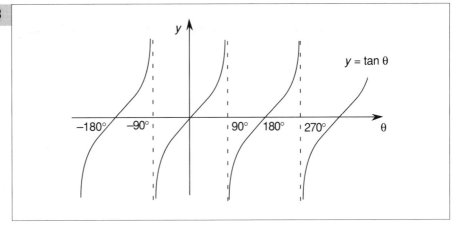

Tan θ is also a periodic function, but its period is 180° rather than the 360° of the other two (or π in radians). Again it has rotational symmetry: it is an *odd* function. You may notice that the gradient of the curve at 0 is 1, unlike the graph of, say, $y = x^3$ which has a gradient of 0 at the origin.

Here's a table to summarise the properties of the three functions. (The value of the angle θ has been restricted to the range of $0 \le \theta < 360°$.)

Table 7.1

	sin θ	cos θ	tan θ
max value	1	1	Can take any value
when θ =	90°	0	positive or negative
min. value	−1	−1	Can take any value
when θ =	270°	180°	positive or negative
symmetries	Rotational	y-axis	Rotational
	ODD	EVEN	ODD
periodic	YES	YES	YES
period	360°	360°	180°

Transformations of the graphs

The properties of the sine and cosine curves (that they have a small range and are periodic) make them very suitable graphs to show the effects of the standard transformations and combinations of these. We'll take $y = \sin x$ as an example but it could equally well be $y = \cos x$.

y= a + sin x

As we know, this is a translation of a in the y-direction, e.g. $y = 2 + \sin x$ is the graph of $y = \sin x$ moved up 2 units:

Figure 7.14

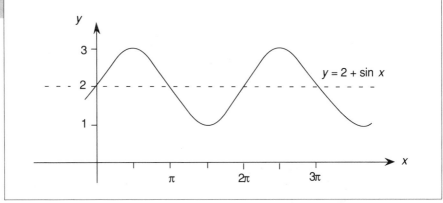

The graph passes through the y-axis at $(0, 2)$ and has a range of $1 \le y \le 3$: its maximum is at the same x-coordinates but the value is different.

y = sin (x + a)

This is a translation of $-a$ in the x-direction, e.g. $y = \sin\left(x + \frac{\pi}{3}\right)$ is the graph of $y = \sin x$ moved back $\frac{\pi}{3}$.

Figure 7.15

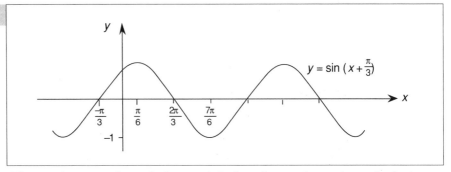

The graph passes through the y-axis before the maximum is reached – its range is still $-1 \le y \le 1$: the maximum has the same value but the x-coordinates of these points are different.

y = a sin x

A scaling factor a in the y-direction, e.g. $y = 2 \sin x$ is the graph of $y = \sin x$ stretched upwards and downwards:

Figure 7.16

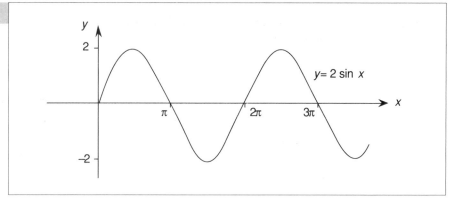

The period is unchanged, but the range has doubled – it is now $-2 \le y \le 2$.

y = sin (ax)

A scaling, factor $\frac{1}{a}$ in the x-direction, e.g. $y = \sin(2x)$ is the graph of $y = \sin x$ squeezed in the x-direction by $\frac{1}{2}$.

Figure 7.17

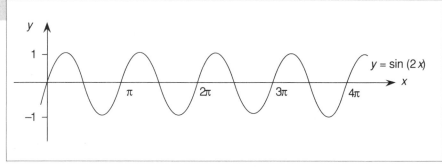

The range is still the same, but the period has now changed – it is half of what it was, i.e. it is now π.

Combinations of transformations

Once you're familiar with these basic transformations, you can have a go at applying a succession of them. Here's an example using three ...

Example

Sketch the graph of $y = 1 + 2\sin\left(x - \frac{\pi}{4}\right)$ for values of x between 0 and 2π, giving the coordinates of the maximum and minimum points.

Solution	We'll work from the transformations nearest the x first of all, so that in order it will be:

$$\sin x \xrightarrow{\text{Forward } \frac{\pi}{4}} \sin\left(x-\frac{\pi}{4}\right) \xrightarrow[y\text{-direction}]{\text{Stretch}} 2\sin\left(x-\frac{\pi}{4}\right) \xrightarrow{\text{Up 1}} 1+2\sin\left(x-\frac{\pi}{4}\right)$$

The corresponding graphs will be:

Figure 7.18

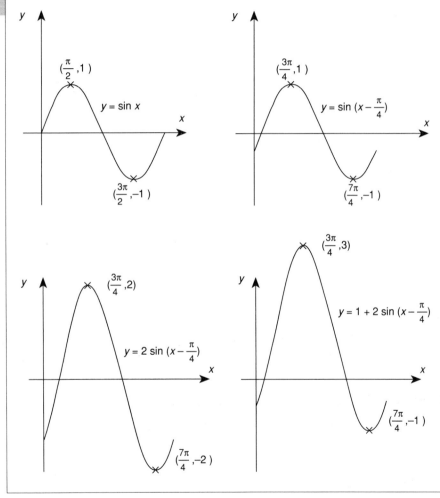

You should now be able to answer Exercise 4 on p. 104.

Equivalent angles

We mentioned before that the trigonometric functions are examples of *many to one functions*; that different angles from the domain give the same value in the range (this means that as they stand, the functions do not have inverses). If we look at the graph of sin *x*, we can investigate which angles give the same value.

Figure 7.19

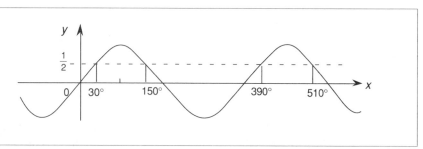

We know that the period of sin *x* is 360° or 2π, so sin 30° is the same as sin (360° + 30°) = sin 390° and sin (360° + 390°) = sin 750° and so on. There is one other angle between 0 and 360° which gives the same value as sin 30°. Since the graph is symmetrical about *x* = 90°, this other angle is as much *above* 90° as 30° is *below* 90°, i.e. it is 150°. As you can see from looking at the graph, this is the same as saying that the angle is as much below 180° as 30° is above 0, which gives the same answer. We can write this as a formula:

$$\sin(180° - \theta) = \sin\theta$$

Again from the graph we can see that because of the rotational symmetry, sin (–30°) is the same as –sin 30° and also, given the symmetry about *x* = 90°, sin (–30°) is the same as sin 210°.

Figure 7.20

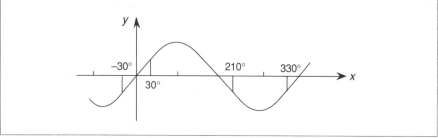

We can express this as   sin (–30°)   = –sin 30°

                              sin (180° + 30°) = –sin 30°

and as we can see   sin (360° – 30°) = –sin 30°

                              and so on.

If we change the signs on both sides of the last two, we have
$-\sin(180° + 30°) = \sin 30°$ and $-\sin(360° - 30°) = \sin 30°$.
Collecting these together, we end up with ...

$$
\begin{aligned}
\sin \theta &= \sin(180° - \theta) \\
&= -\sin(180° + \theta) \\
&= -\sin(360° - \theta) \\
&= \sin(360° + \theta) \\
&= \ldots
\end{aligned}
$$

Perhaps you would like to look at the graph of $y = \cos x$ and check that the following table, written in radians for practice, is correct ...

$$
\begin{aligned}
\cos \theta &= -\cos(\pi - \theta) \\
&= -\cos(\pi + \theta) \\
&= \cos(2\pi - \theta) \\
&= \cos(2\pi + \theta) \\
&= \ldots
\end{aligned}
$$

and finally the least complicated one, $y = \tan x$:

$$
\begin{aligned}
\tan \theta &= -\tan(\pi - \theta) \\
&= \tan(\pi + \theta) \\
&= \ldots
\end{aligned}
$$

This means that for each of the functions, there will be two angles between 0 and 360° (or 0 and 2π in radians) that give the same positive value and two angles in the same domain that give the same value but negative.

For example: $\sin 30° = \dfrac{1}{2} \Rightarrow \sin(180° - 30°) = \dfrac{1}{2}$

i.e. $\sin 150° = \dfrac{1}{2}$

$\Rightarrow \sin(180° + 30°) = -\dfrac{1}{2}$

i.e. $\quad \sin 210° = -\dfrac{1}{2}$

$\Rightarrow \quad \sin (360° - 30°) \;=\; -\dfrac{1}{2}$

i.e. $\quad \sin 330° = -\dfrac{1}{2}$

In addition, we can add 360° onto each of these angles without changing the corresponding value:

e.g. $\quad \sin 150° \;=\; \sin (360° + 150°) \;=\; \sin 510° \;=\; \dfrac{1}{2}$

and $\quad \sin 210° \;=\; \sin (360° + 210°) \;=\; \sin 570° \;=\; -\dfrac{1}{2}$

You should now be able to answer Exercises 5 and 6 on p. 104.

Solving trigonometric equations

In the previous work we saw how each of the basic trigonometric functions have equivalent angles, i.e. different angles which give the same value. For example, the sine of the angles θ, $180° - \theta$ and $360° + \theta$ all have the same value. With such a choice available we have to look carefully at the question and see the limits within which the angles must lie. If the question asks for the solution of $\sin \theta = \dfrac{1}{2}$, we can find one value for θ which satisfies this: $\theta = 30°$, and then deduce some further values,

e.g. $180° - \theta = 150°$ and $360° + \theta = 390°$ which are also solutions.

The given limits then determine which, if any, of these are suitable: we may have to go further back, by subtracting multiples of 360° from the solutions, or further forward, by adding multiples of 360°. Standard limits include $0 \le x \le 360°$, $-180° < x \le 180°$ and $0 \le \theta \le 180°$, but the question may ask for solutions within a different range.

Quadrants

The axes are divided into four quadrants:

Figure 7.21

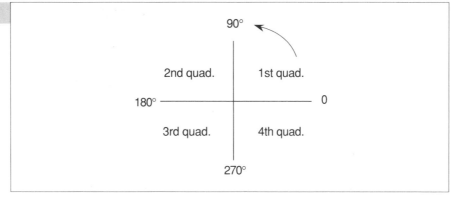

as the angle increases anticlockwise. If we look at the graphs of the trigonometric ratios, we see that sine is positive between 0 and 180°, i.e. in the first and second quadrants, cosine is positive between 0 and 90°, and 270° and 360°, i.e. in the first and fourth quadrants, and tan is positive between 0 and 90°, and 180° and 270°, in the first and third quadrants.

Gathering together the signs of the three ratios in the various quadrants we can put them in the following diagram:

Figure 7.22

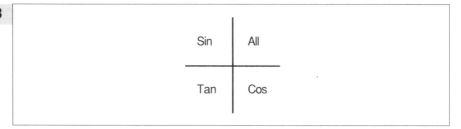

We can simplify this by including only those ratios which are positive in any particular quadrant, i.e.:

Figure 7.23

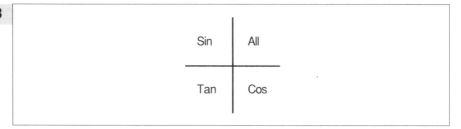

This can be remembered as 'All Stations To Coventry' (or similar), the initial letters as you move round anti-clockwise.

In summary, the method for solving trigonometric equations is

1   quadrants

2   principal angle

3   angles

4   correction (for range).

We'll have a look at an example and see how the method works in practice.

Example   Solve the equation $\cos\theta = -\dfrac{1}{2}$ for values of θ in the range $-180° < \theta < 180°$

Solution   *Quadrants:*   since $\cos\theta$ is negative, θ must be in quadrants 2 and 3.

Principal angle: means ignoring any minus sign and finding the acute angle for which $\cos\theta = \dfrac{1}{2}$. From your calculator, this is $60°$

Angles: The principal angle is always added onto or subtracted from angles on the x-axis, i.e. $180° \pm$ (angle) or $360° -$ (angle) (and not, for example, $90° +$ (angle) or $270° -$ (angle). In this case, in the 2nd and 3rd quadrants we want $180° -$ (angle), i.e. $180° - 60° = 120°$ and $180° +$ (angle), i.e. $180° + 60° = 240°$.

Correction: The solution $\theta = 120°$ is within the required range whereas $\theta = 240°$ is too large. In this case, we have to subtract multiples of $360°$ until the angle falls within the stated values. $240° - 360° = -120°$ and this is the second solution.

In fact, since $\cos\theta$ is an *even* function, i.e. $\cos\theta = \cos(-\theta)$, the solutions will always occur in pairs, $\pm$ (angle).

We'll try a further example:

Example   Solve the equation $\tan\theta = \dfrac{1}{\sqrt{3}}$ for values of θ in the range $0 < \theta < 2\pi$.

Solution   *Quadrants:* $\tan\theta > 0 \Rightarrow \theta$ is in 1 or 3

Principal angle: inverse $\tan\dfrac{1}{\sqrt{3}} = 30°$

Angles: $30°$ is one solution. In the third quadrant, $180° + 30° = 210°$ is the other.

Correction: Note that the range is given in *radians*: you would lose a mark if you gave the solution in degrees. You can work with radians from the beginning or work in degrees and convert later. If, however, the angle is not a whole number of degrees you can put your calculator in radian mode, remembering that the solutions are now $\pi \pm$ (angle) or $2\pi -$ (angle).

To return to the present example, we have $30°$ and $210°$, i.e. $\dfrac{\pi}{6}$ and $\pi + \dfrac{\pi}{6} = \dfrac{7\pi}{6}$. These are both within the stated range and are the solutions.

Equations with composite angles

These are equations like $\sin 2x = \dfrac{\sqrt{3}}{2}$ or $\tan(x - 50°) = -1$ where the argument is more complicated than just x. We can make a simple substitution, like $y = 2x$ or $y = x - 50°$, solve this for y and deduce the appropriate values for x. There can be a change in the number of solutions so we have to be careful. Let's solve each of the equations above for values of x within the range $0 < x < 360°$.

$$\sin 2x = \frac{\sqrt{3}}{2}: \text{put } y = 2x \Rightarrow \sin y = \frac{\sqrt{3}}{2}$$

Sin positive falls in quadrants 1 and 2 and the principal angle is $60°$. In the first quadrant the value is $60°$, in the second $180° - 60° = 120°$. But now, since we are going to divide these values by 2, we can afford to increase each of these by $360°$ to give altogether $y = 60°, 120°, 420°$ or $480°$.

Putting back $y = 2x$, $2x = 60°, 120°, 420°$ or $480°$

$\Rightarrow$ $x = 30°, 60°, 210°$ or $240°$

These are all within the range given.

Tan $(x - 50°) = -1$:   Put $y = x - 50° \Rightarrow \tan y = -1$

Tan is negative in quadrants 2 and 4, and the principal angle is $45°$. In 2, $180° - 45° = 135°$. In 4, $360° - 45° = 315°$.

$\Rightarrow$ $y = 135°$ or $315°$

Putting $y = x - 50°$, $x - 50° = 135°$ or $315°$

$x = 185°$ or $365°$

The first of these is within the range: the second is too large and we have to subtract $360°$ to give a final solution of $x = 5°$ or $185°$

You should now be able to answer Exercises 7, 8, 9 and 10 on p. 104.

EXERCISES

1 Express in radians:

a 360° **b** 60° **c** 270° **d** 540° **e** 150° **f** 15° **g** 75° **h** 225°

i 315° **j** 135°

2 Express in degrees:

a $\dfrac{\pi}{3}$ **b** $\dfrac{3\pi}{4}$ **c** $\dfrac{2\pi}{3}$ **d** $\dfrac{5\pi}{6}$ **e** $\dfrac{3\pi}{2}$ **f** 4π **g** $\dfrac{5\pi}{4}$ **h** $\dfrac{7\pi}{6}$ **i** $\dfrac{5\pi}{3}$ **j** $\dfrac{\pi}{10}$

radians.

3 Find the arc lengths and areas of sectors subtending an angle of:

a   90°   with radius 4 cm

b   210°   with radius 12 cm

c $\dfrac{3\pi}{4}$ with radius 8 cm

d $\dfrac{5\pi}{3}$ with radius 9 cm

4 Sketch the graphs for $0 \le x \le 360°$ if:

a $y = (\sin x) - 2$ **b** $y = \cos(x + 60°)$ **c** $y = \tan(x - 45°)$

d $y = 2\cos(x - 30°)$ **e** $y = -\cos x$

5 Find 3 additional angles in the interval $0 \le x \le 720°$ for which:

a $\sin x = -0.5$ (first angle is $180° + 30° = 210°$)

b $\cos x = 0.8$ (first angle is 36.9°)

c $\tan x = 4$ (first angle is 76.0°)

Give your answers to 1 decimal place where necessary.

6 Find two angles in the interval $0 < x < 2\pi$ for which:

a $\sin x = 0.8$

b $\cos x = 0.4$

c $\tan x = -2.5$

Give your answers in radians correct to 2 decimal places.

7 Solve the equations in Question 6 in the new interval $-180° < x < 180°$, giving your answer in degrees to 1 decimal place.

8 Find the values of θ between 0 and 360° such that:

a $\sin 2\theta = 0.3$ **b** $\cos 2\theta = -0.5$ **c** $\tan 2\theta = -1$

giving your answer in degrees to 1 decimal place (where necessary)

9 Solve the equation $\cos(x - 10°) = \dfrac{1}{2}$ for values of x in the range

$-180° < x < 180°$

10 Solve the equation $\tan(2\theta + \dfrac{\pi}{4}) = -1$ for values of θ

in the range $0 < \theta < \pi$.

SUMMARY

This section has been an introduction to a very important group of functions, their graphs and related equations. Make sure you are able to change from radians to degrees and the other way round – and to think in radians when necessary!

$$\tan \emptyset = -1 \qquad 2\emptyset + \frac{\pi}{4} = \emptyset.$$

$$\emptyset = \frac{\pi 5}{4} + \pi n$$

$$= -\frac{\pi}{2} + \pi n$$

$$= -\frac{\pi}{4} - 1$$

8

Differentiation

No matter where we choose to measure it, the gradient of a straight line is always the same. When we look at any other line, we can see that the gradient changes as we move from one point on the line to another. To find the gradient at a particular point from the equation of the curve we use a technique called differentiation: the subject of this section.

One of the 'interesting' points in a graph is when the curve stops going up and starts to go down (or the other way round). In this section we're also going to learn how to locate these points by differentiating. This is useful when we want to make an accurate sketch of a curve or to maximise or minimise the value of some variable that is subject to a limiting condition.

The gradient at a point

First of all, let's think what we mean when we say the gradient at a point. How is this possible? We can have the gradient of a line joining two points:

Figure 8.1

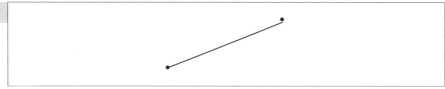

but we cannot find a single gradient for a point on its own:

Figure 8.2

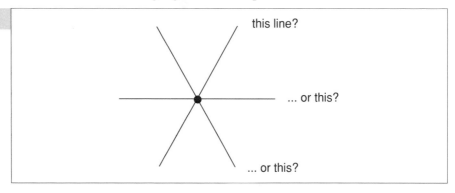

So there's the puzzle … we need two points to find the gradient – but we want the gradient at just one point. To resolve this, we introduce a mathematical helper: something which appears, puts us on the right track and disappears again.

The helper in this case is another point on the curve. We join this point and our original point so that we now have a line and a gradient – and then we shrink the distance between the two points to zero. Only one point is left – but we still have the line. Its gradient is the gradient of the curve at that point.

Let's take an example of this, the function

$$y = x^2$$

and suppose that we want the gradient at the point (x,y) shown on Figure 8.3. We'll take another point a little further along; x has increased to $x + \delta x$ and y to $y + \delta y$ where we use δ to indicate a small change in x or y. This point $(x + \delta x, y + \delta y)$ is also on the curve $y = x^2$, so we can say that:

$$\begin{aligned} y + \delta y \quad &= \quad (x + \delta x)^2 \\ &= \quad x^2 + 2x\,\delta x + \delta x^2 \end{aligned}$$

But since $y = x^2$, $\delta y \quad = \quad 2x\,\delta x + \delta x^2$ [1]

Figure 8.3

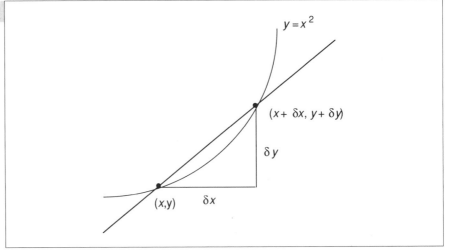

The gradient of the line joining the two points is then:

$$\frac{y\text{ increase}}{x\text{ increase}} = \frac{\delta y}{\delta x} = \frac{2x\,\delta x + \delta x^2}{\delta x} \qquad \text{from} \quad [1]$$

$$= \quad 2x + \delta x \qquad\qquad [2]$$

We have the gradient a little to the right of the point where we want it, so now we bring the second point closer and closer by saying that δx, the increase in x, becomes smaller and smaller – until it eventually disappears.

We say in this case that 'δx tends to zero' and write $\delta x \to 0$. When this has happened, the ratio $\dfrac{\delta y}{\delta x}$ is written as $\dfrac{dy}{dx}$.

Then
$$\frac{\delta y}{\delta x} = 2x + \delta x \qquad\qquad [2]$$

becomes, as $\delta x \to 0$, $\dfrac{dy}{dx} = 2x$

This is the gradient function for the equation $y = x^2$. Knowing this, we can immediately say what the gradient is at any point on the curve, for example:

when $x = 4$,   the gradient, $\dfrac{dy}{dx} = 2 \times 4 = 8$

$x = -3$, $\dfrac{dy}{dx} = -6$

$x = 0$, $\dfrac{dy}{dx} = 0$ etc.

In order to clarify this process we will examine the gradient between the point (2,4) on the curve $y = x^2$ and a second point on that curve.

Suppose at the second point, $x = 2.1$. Then $y = x^2 = (2.1)^2 = 4.41$.

The gradient between the points (2,4) and (2.1, 4.41) is:

Figure 8.4

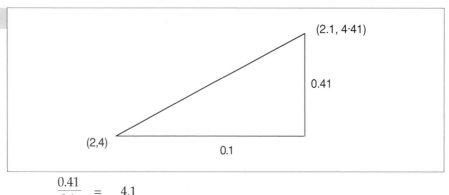

$$\frac{0.41}{0.1} = 4.1$$

which is quite close to the answer that we obtained above.

Can you see that the ratio of the increases in y and x, the gradient, tends to a certain value as the increase in x tends to zero?

The value is just a little more than 4, but the closer we bring the second point to the point where $x = 2$, the closer the gradient is to 4. We say that in the limit, the gradient at the point $x = 2$ is 4 (because we can make it as close to 4 as we like by choosing a suitable value of x).

You should now be able to answer Exercise 1 on p. 119.

Gradient function for other powers of x

In a similar fashion, we can find out the gradient function for the curve $y = x^3$. If we take the point (x, y) and a second point on the curve close to this, say $(x + \delta x, y + \delta y)$, then since this second point lies on the curve $y = x^3$,

$$y + \delta y = (x + \delta x)^3$$
$$= x^3 + 3x^2\delta x + 3x\delta x^2 + \delta x^3$$

But $y = x^3$, so
$$\delta y = 3x^2\delta x + 3x\delta x^2 + \delta x^3$$

Divide by δx
$$\frac{\delta y}{\delta x} = 3x^2 + 3x\delta x + \delta x^2$$

In the limit, as $\delta x \to 0$, $\dfrac{\delta y}{\delta x} \to 3x^2$, with the other terms involving δx disappearing. We write this:

> If $y = x^3$, then the gradient function $\dfrac{dy}{dx} = 3x^2$

We could repeat this procedure for any value of the power of x and we would find the general result that:

> The gradient function of the curve $y = x^n$ where n is rational
> is given by $\dfrac{dy}{dx} = nx^{n-1}$

So for example,

if   **a** $y = x^5$, then $\dfrac{dy}{dx} = 5x^4$

     b $y = x^{-2}$, $\dfrac{dy}{dx} = -2x^{-3}$

     c $y = x^{\frac{1}{3}}$ $\dfrac{dy}{dx} = \dfrac{1}{3}x^{-\frac{2}{3}}$

Properties of gradients

1   If the functions are added or subtracted, the gradients are added or subtracted:

     d $y = x^4 + x^{-4}$ then $\dfrac{dy}{dx} = 4x^3 - 4x^{-5}$

     e $y = x^7 - x^{-2}$ then $\dfrac{dy}{dx} = 7x^6 - (-2x^{-3}) = 7x^6 + 2x^{-3}$

2   Constants in front of the functions appear in front of the gradients:

$$\mathbf{f} \quad y = 5x^3 = 5(x^3)$$

$$\frac{dy}{dx} = 5(3x^2) = 15x^2$$

and $$\mathbf{g} \quad y = -2x^{-\frac{1}{2}}$$

$$\frac{dy}{dx} = -2\left(-\frac{1}{2}x^{-\frac{3}{2}}\right) = x^{-\frac{3}{2}}$$

3   Constants on their own disappear:

$$\mathbf{h} \quad y = 6x^2 + \frac{6}{x^2} + 2 = 6x^2 + 6x^{-2} + 2$$

$$\frac{dy}{dx} = 12x - 12x^{-3}$$

You can probably see from the above example how we're going to treat functions that are given in a different form, for instance:

$$\frac{6}{x^2}, \quad \frac{5}{x^{\frac{1}{2}}}, \quad \sqrt{x}, \quad \sqrt[3]{x^2}$$

We use our knowledge of indices to write them in the standard form, and then differentiate:

$$y = \frac{6}{x^2} = 6x^{-2} \text{ (as above)} \Rightarrow \frac{dy}{dx} = -12x^{-3}$$

$$y = \frac{5}{x^{\frac{1}{2}}} = 5x^{-\frac{1}{2}} \Rightarrow \frac{dy}{dx} = -\frac{5}{2}x^{-\frac{3}{2}}$$

$$y = \sqrt{x} = x^{\frac{1}{2}} \Rightarrow \frac{dy}{dx} = \frac{1}{2}x^{-\frac{1}{2}}$$

$$y = \sqrt[3]{x^2} = x^{\frac{2}{3}} \Rightarrow \frac{dy}{dx} = \frac{2}{3}x^{-\frac{1}{3}}$$

When you've had a bit of practice you should find them reasonably easy.

If we have to differentiate fairly simple products, like $y = (3x + 2)(x^2 - 1)$ or $\sqrt{x}\,(x^2 + 2)$, we multiply out first of all and then differentiate

$$y = (3x + 2)(x^2 - 1) \qquad\qquad y = \sqrt{x}\,(x^2 + 2) = x^{\frac{1}{2}}(x^2 + 2)$$

$$= 3x^3 + 2x^2 - 3x - 2 \qquad\qquad\qquad = x^{\frac{5}{2}} + 2x^{\frac{1}{2}}$$

$$\Rightarrow \frac{dy}{dx} = 9x^2 - 4x - 3 \qquad\qquad \Rightarrow \frac{dy}{dx} = \frac{5}{2}x^{\frac{3}{2}} + x^{-\frac{1}{2}}$$

You should now be able to answer Exercises 2 and 3 on pp. 119–120.

Maximum and minimum points

As we've seen, a curve does not have a fixed gradient: at any particular point the gradient has the same value as the gradient of the tangent to the curve at the same point.

The gradient of a curve $y = f(x)$ is written $\frac{dy}{dx}$ or $f'(x)$. It tells us what is happening to y as x increases: if the gradient is positive, y is increasing, if negative, y is decreasing. Let's have a look at part of a curve with tangents drawn in at different points ...

Figure 8.5

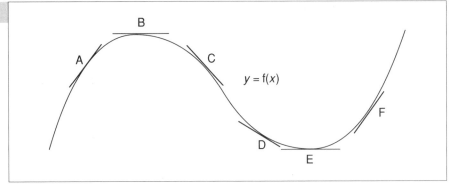

At the point A, the gradient is positive and at C it is negative. At some point in between, B, the gradient is *zero*. This is called a *maximum point* (although only a local maximum – there may be other regions where the value of the function is greater).

Similarly, at D the gradient is still negative, at F positive and at some point E, the gradient is zero: this is a *minimum point*.

At maximum or minimum points, the gradient is zero, i.e. $\frac{dy}{dx} = 0$

Distinguishing between maximum and minimum

Anything in the form $\frac{d\ \ }{dx}$ means how $\ \ $ is changing as x increases.

$\frac{dy}{dx}$ means how y is changing as x increases and $\frac{d(\frac{dy}{dx})}{dx}$ means how $\frac{dy}{dx}$

or the gradient is changing as x increases. Since $\frac{d(\frac{dy}{dx})}{dx}$ looks a bit cumbersome, it is written $\frac{d^2y}{dx^2}$.

$\dfrac{dy}{dx}$ means how y is changing as x increases

$\dfrac{d^2y}{dx^2}$ means how $\dfrac{dy}{dx}$ is changing as x increases

Now let's have a look back at our curve and see how the gradient changes as x increases:

A gradient positive
B gradient zero   } gradient is decreasing as x increases, i.e. $\dfrac{d^2y}{dx^2} < 0$
C gradient negative

D gradient negative
E gradient zero   } gradient is increasing as x increases, i.e. $\dfrac{d^2y}{dx^2} > 0$
F gradient positive

$\dfrac{d^2y}{dx^2} < 0 \implies$ a maximum point

$\dfrac{d^2y}{dx^2} > 0 \implies$ a minimum point

We now have a method for finding maximum and minimum points and distinguishing between them.

1   Given $y = f(x)$, we differentiate to find $\dfrac{dy}{dx}$

2   We put $\dfrac{dy}{dx} = 0$ and solve this equation for x

3   We put the value of x into f(x) to find the y coordinate

4   We differentiate $\dfrac{dy}{dx}$ to find $\dfrac{d^2y}{dx^2}$

5   We put the value from (2) into $\dfrac{d^2y}{dx^2}$: if this is negative, the point is maximum, if positive, minimum.

Let's see how this works …

Example   Find the coordinates of the turning points for the curve:

$$y \quad = \quad x^3 - 3x$$

Solution   To find the gradient at any point, we differentiate:

$$\frac{dy}{dx} = 3x^2 - 3$$

We want to find the points where the gradient is 0, i.e.:

$$3x^2 - 3 = 0$$

Then $x^2 \;=\; 1 \Rightarrow x \;=\; \pm 1$

When $x = 1,$ $y = 1 - 3 \;=\; -2$

        $x = -1,$ $y = -1 + 3 \;=\; 2$

So the two turning points are $(1, -2)$ and $(-1, 2)$.

Now differentiating $\dfrac{dy}{dx}$ gives:

$$\frac{d^2y}{dx^2} = 6x$$

when $x = 1,$ $\dfrac{d^2y}{dx^2} = 6 > 0$ $\Rightarrow$ minimum

       $x = -1,$ $\dfrac{d^2y}{dx^2} = -6 < 0 \Rightarrow$ maximum

So the turning points are $(1, -2)$ minimum and $(-1, 2)$ maximum.

Another method of determining whether a point is a maximum or minimum (or neither), is to find the sign of the gradient on either side of the point in question. If the gradient is positive just before the point and negative just after.

Figure 8.6

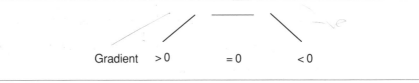

Gradient > 0 $= 0$ < 0

the point is a maximum, and similarly negative before and positive after

Figure 8.7

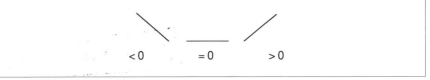

< 0 $= 0$ > 0

means a minimum point. Let's take an example of this:

Example   Find the turning point of the curve $y = x^4 - 1$ and determine its nature.

Solution

We differentiate, $\frac{dy}{dx} = 4x^3$ and put the gradient equal to zero $\Rightarrow 4x^3 = 0 \Rightarrow$ $x = 0$.

When x is slightly less than zero, at -0.1 say, the gradient $\frac{dy}{dx} = 4(-0.1)^3 < 0$.

When x is slightly greater than zero, at $+0.1$ say, the gradient

$\frac{dy}{dx} = 4(0.1)^3 > 0$

Figure 8.8

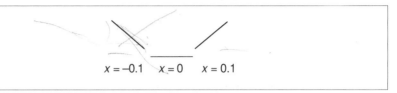

$x = -0.1 \quad x = 0 \quad x = 0.1$

The point is a *minimum* point. (Note that $\frac{d^2y}{dx^2} = 12x^2$ and at the point $x = 0$ this would be zero, so we could not use the first method in this case.)

If the gradient has the same sign on either side of the point where the gradient is zero (the *stationary* point), the point is called a *point of inflection*.

Figure 8.9

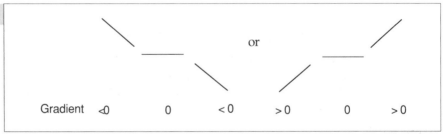

or

Gradient $\quad <0 \qquad 0 \qquad <0 \qquad >0 \qquad 0 \qquad >0$

For example, the curve $y = x^3$ has a stationary point when $x = 0$. The gradient $\frac{dy}{dx} = 3x^2$ and this is positive either side of $x = 0$, so the stationary point is a point of inflection.

Figure 8.10

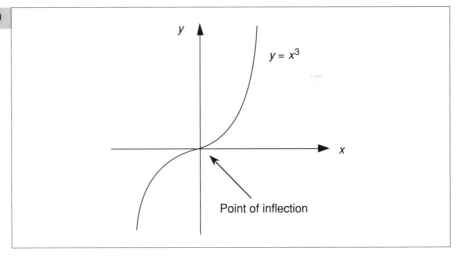

You should now be able to answer Exercise 4 on p. 120.

Increasing and decreasing functions

Some graphs have a positive gradient throughout like:

Figure 8.11

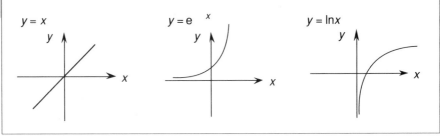

These are called *increasing functions*. Similarly, some graphs have a negative gradient throughout:

Figure 8.12

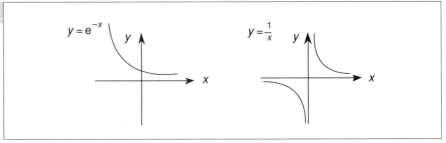

and these are called, as you may be able to guess, *decreasing* functions. They have no turning points, since the gradient is never zero, and consequently they all have *inverses*.

Differentiating e^x and ln$x$

The function $y = e^x$ has a unique property – when we differentiate it we get the same thing that we started with, i.e. $\frac{dy}{dx} = e^x$. We shall be looking more at this and other functions, but for the moment we shall just mention this and the differential of ln$x$. If $y = \ln x$, then $\frac{dy}{dx} = \frac{1}{x}$.

Finally, to round off this brief introduction to further differentiation, if $y = e^{ax}$ where a is a constant, then $\frac{dy}{dx} = ae^{ax}$.

> If $y = e^x$ then $\frac{dy}{dx} = e^x$
>
> $y = \ln x$ then $\frac{dy}{dx} = \frac{1}{x}$
>
> $y = e^{ax}$ then $\frac{dy}{dx} = ae^{ax}$

Let's look at a couple of examples of these:

Example Differentiate the following with respect to x:

a $e^x + x^2$ **b** $2e^x$ **c** e^{3x} **d** $x + \ln x$

Solution

a $y = e^x + x^2$ We differentiate term by term.

$\frac{dy}{dx} = e^x + 2x$

b $y = 2e^x$ We differentiate and multiply by the constant.

$\frac{dy}{dx} = 2e^x$

c $y = e^{3x}$ We bring the constant down in front, otherwise unchanged.

$\frac{dy}{dx} = 3e^{3x}$

d $y = x + \ln x$ Differentiate term by term.

$\frac{dy}{dx} = 1 + \frac{1}{x}$

You should now be able to answer Exercise 5 on p. 120.

Maximum and minimum problems

These problems could probably be summarised as 'making the most of available resources'. Suppose I have a piece of wire 40 cm long. If I make a rectangle from the wire, how should I choose the length and breadth to give me the greatest possible area? I could choose the length to be 15 cm and the breadth 4 cm.

Figure 8.13

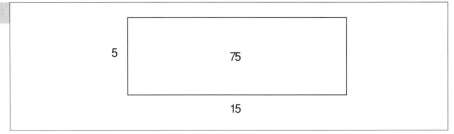

This gives me the correct perimeter of 40 cm: the area would be $5 \times 15 = 75 \text{ cm}^2$.

Another possibility would be 8 cm by 12 cm.

Figure 8.14

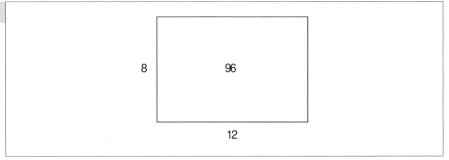

This would give an area of 96 cm², an improvement on the last attempt.

If I want to try and put the problem in mathematical terms, I need to give the variables names, so we can call the breadth x cm, the length y cm and the area A cm².

Figure 8.15

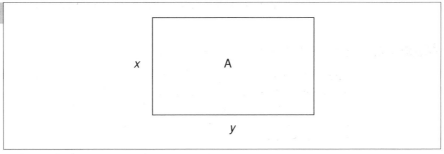

Now there are two quantities: one fixed, the perimeter, and the other varying, the area. We can express these as equations in x and y:

| perimeter: | $2x + 2y$ | $= 40$ | [1] |
| area: | xy | $= A$ | [2] |

(handwritten notes in right margin)
$2x + 2y = 40$
$A = xy$
$y = \frac{A}{x}$

The strategy is to express the quantity that is varying in terms of only one variable. To do this, we need to make the other variable the subject of the fixed equation. In this case, it doesn't really matter which variable we take, but we'll take y:

$$2y = 40 - 2x$$

(divide by 2) $\quad y = 20 - x \qquad$ [3]

(handwritten)
$2x + \frac{2A}{x} = 40.$
$x + \frac{A}{x} = 20$

we now substitute this expression into equation [2], which gives:

$$x(20 - x) = A$$

(handwritten) $x^2 + A = 20x.$

If we turn this round and multiply out the bracket:

$$A = 20x - x^2$$

(handwritten) $x^2 - 20x = A.$

we have now expressed the quantity that can vary in terms of just one of the variables.

(handwritten) $2x - 20 = A.$

We can now use our method for finding maximum and minimum values of a function – we differentiate our expression for A with respect to x and equate the result to zero.

(handwritten) $x = 10$

$$\frac{dA}{dx} = 20 - 2x = 0$$

$$2x = 20$$

$$\Rightarrow \quad x = 10 \qquad [4]$$

When we put this value back into equation [3], we find that

$$y = 20 - 10 = 10$$

So the rectangle which encloses the maximum area is a square of side 10 cm and this maximum area is 100 cm^2. (We could actually have enclosed a bigger area if we had used a circle with a perimeter of 40 cm. What would have been the area in this case?)

\Here is another example, a little more difficult this time, but you will see that the basic pattern of the solution is the same.

Example A solid right circular cylinder has a fixed volume of 1000 cm^3. Show that the total surface area A cm^2 of the cylinder is related to the base radius x cm of the cylinder by the equation:

$$A = 2\pi x^2 + \frac{2000}{x}$$

Given that x varies, show that A is a minimum when $x^3 = \frac{500}{\pi}$.

Find the minimum value of A, giving your answer to 1 decimal place.

Solution A right circular cylinder means that the sides are at right-angles to the base. In all these questions, it probably helps to draw a diagram and mark in some lengths:

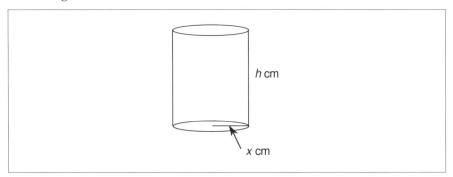

Since we're not told the height, we can call it h cm. We're looking for two quantities, one fixed and one varying. In this case the fixed quantity is the volume, which for a cylinder is $\pi x^2 h$ cm^3 where x cm is the radius of the base. The quantity which varies, the surface area, is made up of two parts: $2\pi xh$ cm^2 for the curved surface and $2 \times \pi x^2$ cm^2 for the top and bottom. Our two equations are:

$$V = \pi x^2 h = 1000 \text{ (given)} \quad [1]$$
$$A = 2\pi xh + 2\pi x^2 \quad [2]$$

We have a choice of making x or h the subject of equation [1]. It's easier to take h, particularly as h only occurs once in the second equation.

From [1] $h = \dfrac{1000}{\pi x^2}$ [3]

and putting this into [2]

$$A = 2\pi x\left(\frac{1000}{\pi x}\right) + 2\pi x^2$$

$$= \frac{2000}{x} + 2\pi x^2$$

i.e. $\quad A = 2\pi x^2 + \dfrac{2000}{x}$ [4]

We can now differentiate this with respect to x, remembering that we can re-write $\dfrac{2000}{x}$ as $2000\, x^{-1}$:

$$\frac{dA}{dx} = 4\pi x - \frac{2000}{x^2}$$

Putting this equal to zero:

$$4\pi x - \frac{2000}{x^2} = 0$$

$$4\pi x = \frac{2000}{x^2}$$

$$4\pi x^3 = 2000$$

$$x^3 = \frac{2000}{4\pi} = \frac{500}{\pi} \quad \text{as required.}$$

To show that this is a minimum, we need to find $\dfrac{d^2 A}{dx^2}$ and show that it's positive when x has this value.

$$\frac{d^2 A}{dx^2} = 4\pi + \frac{4000}{x^3}$$

We can see this is positive without working out the exact value.

Using a calculator, we find that $x = 5.419$ (3 decimal places) and when we put this value into equation [4] we get A = 553.6, the required minimum value.

You should now be able to answer Exercises 6, 7 and 8 on pp. 120–121.

EXERCISES

1 Calculate the gradient between the point (2,4) and the point on the curve $y = x^2$ where x is

    a 2.01   **b** 2.001   **c** 2.0000001

2 Differentiate:

    a $3x^2$ **b** $4x^4 - 2$ **c** $x + \dfrac{1}{x}$ **d** $\sqrt[4]{x}$ **e** $\sqrt[5]{x} + \dfrac{5}{\sqrt{x}}$

f $\sqrt{x^5}$ **g** $\dfrac{1}{\sqrt[3]{x}}$ **h** $\dfrac{5}{x^4}+1$ **i** $\dfrac{4}{x^{3/4}}$ **j** $\dfrac{x^4+1}{x^2}$ (divide first)

3 Find the value of the gradient at the point indicated for each of the following curves:

a y = $4x^3+2$ at $x=1$

b y = $2x^2-x+1$ at $x=2$

c y = $x^2+\dfrac{1}{x^2}$ at $x=1$

d y = $x^{\frac{3}{2}}-x^{-\frac{3}{2}}$ at $x=4$

e y = $(x+2)^2$ at $x=0$ (multiply out first)

4 Find the turning points and determine their nature for the following curves:

a y = x^2-2x+5

b y = $12x-x^3$

5 Differentiate:

a $3\ln x$ **b** $\ln x - e^x$ **c** $e^{4x}+4$ **d** $3e^{2x}$ **e** $\dfrac{1}{x}+\ln x$

6 For a particular journey of a ship, the running cost, C, in hundreds of pounds, is given in terms of its average speed for the journey, v km h^{-1}, by the equation

$$C = \frac{16\,000}{v} + v^2$$

Use differentiation to calculate the value of v for which C is a minimum, and show that C is a minimum and not a maximum for this value of v.

7 From a large thin plane sheet of metal it is required to make an open rectangular box with a square base so that the box will contain a given volume V. Express the area of the sheet used in terms of V and x, where x is the length of a side of the square base.

Hence find the ratio of the height of the box to x in order that the box consists of a minimum area of the metal sheet.

8 A parcel, in the form of a rectangular block, is held together by three pieces of wire as shown in the diagram. The parcel has square ends of side x cm and is y cm in length. Express the total length of wire in terms of x and y. Given that the total length of tape is 450 cm, express the volume, V cm^3, of the parcel in terms of x. Find the value of x and of y for which V has a stationary value and determine whether this value is a maximum or a minimum.

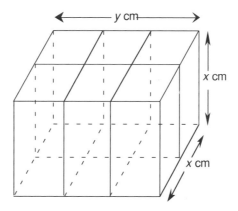

SUMMARY   This section has been concerned with expressing the way one variable changes with another in a formal way – we used this to find the gradient of curves and in particular the position of the maximum and minimum points. Make sure that you can find the differential of simple functions of x like $\sqrt{x}$ and $\dfrac{1}{x}$: later work will depend very much on this activity.

9

Integration

In this section we look at the reverse process of differentiation, called integration, and see how we can derive general formulas for integrating various functions. There will then be an introduction to the application of integration – finding the areas under curves.

The reverse of differentiation

To someone unfamiliar with more advanced maths, the integral sign, written

$$\int$$

looks intriguing. We can look at it as being the opposite of differentiation, so that

$$\int 3x^2 \, dx$$

means quite simply – 'what function do I have to differentiate with respect to x to give $3x^2$?' The answer, as you can probably work out, would be x^3. Having grasped the concept of differentiation, you shouldn't have too much difficulty with this idea – you just have to get used to working things out backwards. After some time, integration becomes a subject in its own right and the connection with differentiation is no longer quite so obvious. For the moment, though, we'll try and keep both operations in mind.

If you can remember, we found a general result for differentiation, that

$$\frac{d(x^n)}{dx} = nx^{n-1}$$

so that, for example, $\dfrac{d(x^7)}{dx} = 7x^6$ and $\dfrac{d(x^{-1/2})}{dx} = -\dfrac{1}{2}x^{-3/2}$

We'll try and find a similar type of formula for integration, starting by working out a few individual results.

Suppose that we want to work out

$$\int x^2 \, dx$$

122

which means finding a function that would give x^2 after differentiation. We know that differentiation would reduce the power by one, so we start by trying x^3. This gives $3x^2$ after differentiation, which is what we want except for the constant. If we try $\frac{1}{3}x^3$, we would have:

$$\frac{d(\frac{1}{3}x^3)}{dx} = \frac{1}{3} \times 3x^2 = x^2$$

which is what we want.

Now let's try to find a function which gives x^4 after differentiation, that is:

$$\int x^4 \, dx$$

Again we start at one power higher : $\frac{d(x^5)}{dx} = 5x^4$, which is too large.

$\frac{d(\frac{1}{5}x^5)}{dx} = \frac{1}{5} \times 5x^4 = x^4$, which is now correct.

You should now be able to answer Exercise 1 on p. 128.

General formula

From the above examples you should begin to see a pattern. If we want to find a function which differentiates to x^n, we have to increase the power by 1 and put the result over the new power, i.e. we differentiate $\frac{x^{n+1}}{n+1}$.

See whether this formula gives you the results that you've already found. It seems to work well – but there's something missing. We could in fact differentiate any of $x^3 + 4$, $x^3 - 2$, $x^3 + \pi$, etc. and still come up with the answer $3x^2$ because any constant tacked onto the main function disappears when you differentiate. Without knowing anything more about particular values of the function, it's not possible to give an exact value to this constant, and so we write $\int x^2 \, dx = \frac{1}{3}x^3 + C$ where C is an arbitrary constant.

This general result is written as:

$$\int x^n dx = \frac{x^{n+1}}{n+1} + C$$

$$(\text{provided } n \neq -1)$$

Try and get into the habit of writing this constant whenever you perform an integration – there doesn't seem to be much point at the moment but later it becomes more important and we will often need to calculate its precise value.

We can use this formula and two other simple rules to work out most simple algebraic integrals. The rules are:

1 Constants may be taken outside the integral, so for example:

$$\int 4x^8\,dx = 4\int x^8\,dx \quad = \quad 4 \times \frac{1}{9}x^9 + C$$

$$= \frac{4}{9}x^9 + C$$

2 The integral of a sum or difference is the same as the sum or difference of the integrals, so that:

$$\int (x^5 + x^7)\,dx \quad = \quad \int x^5\,dx + \int x^7\,dx$$

$$= \frac{1}{6}x^6 + \frac{1}{8}x^8 + C$$

and $$\int \left(x^2 - \frac{1}{x^2}\right)dx \quad = \quad \int x^2\,dx - \int \frac{1}{x^2}dx$$

$$= \frac{1}{3}x^3 - \int x^{-2}\,dx + C$$

$$= \frac{1}{3}x^3 + x^{-1} + C$$

$$= \frac{x^3}{3} + \frac{1}{x} + C$$

You'll see that in the last two examples the two constants from each integral are combined into one constant – we don't need to write something like

$$\frac{1}{6}x^6 + C + \frac{1}{8}x^8 + D \text{ for instance.}$$

Fractions

We can divide through if there is a fraction with a *single* term in the denominator, so that , for example:

$$\int \frac{x^3 + 1}{x^2} \cdot dx = \int \left(\frac{x^3}{x^2} + \frac{1}{x^2}\right)dx = \int \left(x + \frac{1}{x^2}\right)dx$$

$$= \frac{x^2}{2} - \frac{1}{x} + C$$

Note that if the situation is reversed e.g. we have to find $\int \dfrac{x^2}{x^3 + 1}\,dx$

the same method does not hold and we have to use other means.

You should now be able to answer Exercises 2 and 3 on p. 128.

Further integration

The single exception to the rule for integrating x^n is where n = –1, i.e.

$$\int \frac{1}{x}\, dx$$

When we considered differentiation we learned that the differential of $\ln x$ is $\frac{1}{x}$. In fact, we can find quite a few of the 'standard' integrals just by remembering the differentials and reversing:

$$\frac{d(\ln x)}{dx} \;=\; \frac{1}{x} \;\;\Rightarrow\;\; \int \frac{1}{x} dx \;=\; \ln x + C \;\; (x > 0)$$

$$\frac{d(e^x)}{dx} \;=\; e^x \;\;\Rightarrow\;\; \int e^x\, dx \;=\; e^x + C$$

Using this same method, we can work out another slightly more complicated example as well:

$$\frac{d(e^{3x})}{dx} \;=\; 3e^{3x} \;\;\Rightarrow\;\; \int e^{3x}\, dx \;=\; \tfrac{1}{3} e^{3x} + C$$

As with differentiation, the formula involving n holds true when n is a fraction, both positive and negative. So for example:

$$\int \sqrt{x}\; dx \;=\; \int x^{1/2}\, dx \;=\; \frac{1}{\frac{3}{2}} x^{3/2} + C$$

$$= \;\frac{2x^{3/2}}{3} + C$$

and

$$\int \frac{1}{3\sqrt{x}}\, dx \;=\; \int x^{-1/3}\, dx \;=\; \frac{1}{\frac{2}{3}} x^{2/3} + C$$

$$= \;\tfrac{3}{2} x^{2/3} + C$$

and here again we can divide through if there's a single term on the bottom of the fraction, e.g.

$$\int \frac{x+1}{\sqrt{x}} \quad dx \;=\; \int\left(\frac{x}{\sqrt{x}} + \frac{1}{\sqrt{x}}\right) dx \;=\; \int\left(\frac{x^1}{x^{1/2}} + x^{-1/2}\right) dx$$

$$= \;\int (x^{1/2} + x^{-1/2})\, dx$$

$$= \;\tfrac{2}{3} x^{3/2} + 2x^{1/2} + C$$

Before we look at an application of integration, let's make a little table summarising the results so far.

$$\int x^n \, dx \quad = \quad \frac{x^{n+1}}{n+1} + C \qquad [n \neq -1]$$

$$\int \frac{1}{x} \, dx \quad = \quad \ln x + C \qquad (x > 0)$$

$$\int e^x \, dx \quad = \quad e^x + C$$

$$\int e^{ax} \, dx \quad = \quad \frac{1}{a} e^{ax} + C$$

You should now be able to answer Exercise 4 on p. 128.

Definite integrals

Integration can give us the area under curves whose defining function we can integrate. For example, suppose we wanted to find the area under the curve $y = x^2$ bounded by the curve, the x-axis and the lines $x = 1$ and $x = 2$:

Figure 9.1

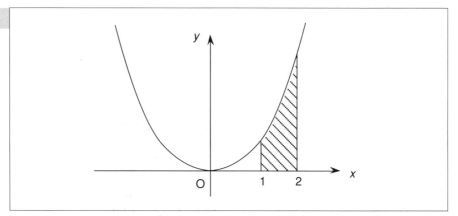

We would write this as $\int_1^2 x^2 dx$, the top limit being the larger of the two values.

When we've found the integral of the function we enclose it in square brackets with the limits at the top and bottom:

$$\int_1^2 x^2 \, dx \quad = \quad \left[\frac{x^3}{3}\right]_1^2$$

Then, to evaluate this, we put in the top value instead of x, $\frac{2^3}{3} = \frac{8}{3}$, and from this subtract the value given by the bottom value instead of x,

i.e. $\frac{1^3}{3} = \frac{1}{3}$

All in all,

$$\int_{1}^{2} x^2\,dx = \left[\frac{x^3}{3}\right]_{1}^{2} = \frac{8}{3} - \frac{1}{3} = \frac{7}{3}$$

which is the area of the shaded region.

Note that when we're using definite integrals the constants are not important because they always disappear in the subtraction. Have a look at another example of this:

Example   Find the area underneath the curve of $y = x^3 - x$ between the points $x = 1$ and $x = 3$.

Solution   The curve of $y = x^3 - x$ looks something like this:

Figure 9.2

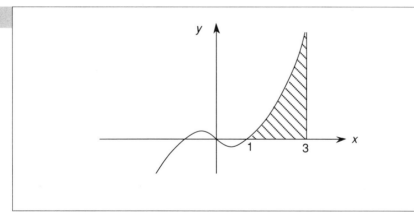

and the shaded portion is the area we want.

This is given by:

$$\int_{1}^{3} y\,dx = \int_{1}^{3}(x^3 - x)\,dx = \left[\frac{x^4}{4} - \frac{x^2}{2}\right]_{1}^{3}$$

$$= \left(\frac{81}{4} - \frac{9}{2}\right) - \left(\frac{1}{4} - \frac{1}{2}\right)$$

$$[\text{when } x = 3] \quad [\text{when } x = 1]$$

$$= \frac{63}{4} + \frac{1}{4} = 16$$

You should now be able to answer Exercise 5, 6, 7 and 8 on pp. 128–129.

EXERCISES

1 Work out:

  a $\dfrac{d(x^4)}{dx}$ and $\int x^3\,dx$

  b $\dfrac{d(x^8)}{dx}$ and $\int x^7\,dx$

  c $\dfrac{d(x^{-2})}{dx}$ and $\int x^{-3}\,dx$

  d $\dfrac{d(4x)}{dx}$ and $\int 5\,dx$

2 Find:

  a $\int 4x^3\,dx$ **b** $\int 2x^4\,dx$ **c** $\int x^4\,dx$ **d** $\int 5x^{-3}\,dx$ **e** $\int \dfrac{6}{x^2}\,dx$

  f $\int (x^3 + 2x)\,dx$ **g** $\int (6x^2 - 5x^4)\,dx$ **h** $\int \left(x^3 + \dfrac{1}{x^3}\right)dx$ **i** $\int \left(\dfrac{x^3 + 1}{x^3}\right)dx$

  j $\int \dfrac{(x+1)^2}{x^4}\,dx$ (multiplying out and then dividing through)

3 **a** $\int x^{3/2}\,dx$ **b** $\int 3x^{2/3}\,dx$ **c** $\int \sqrt{x}\cdot dx$ **d** $\int \dfrac{2}{\sqrt{x}}\cdot dx$

  e $\int (7x^{5/2} - 5x^{3/2})\,dx$ **f** $\int (\sqrt{x} + 1)^2\,dx$ **g** $\int (x^{2/3} - x^{1/2})\,dx$

  h $\int \dfrac{(x+1)^2}{\sqrt{x}}\cdot dx$

4 Integrate the following functions with respect to x and then differentiate your answer to check.

  a e^{2x} **b** e^{-2x} **c** $6e^{-x/2}$ **d** $\dfrac{1}{x}$ **e** $x - \dfrac{2}{x}$

  f $(1 + e^x)^2$ (multiply out first)

5 Evaluate:

  a $\displaystyle\int_0^2 x^4\,dx$

  b $\displaystyle\int_{-1}^0 (x^3 - x)\,dx$

  c $\displaystyle\int_0^1 e^{-x}\,dx$

6 The diagram shows part of the curve with equation $y = x^2 + 4$ between the x-axis, and the lines $x = 2, x = 4$. Find the area of the shaded region.

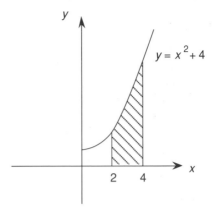

7 Find the area enclosed by the curve with equation $y = x^{\frac{1}{2}}$, the x-axis and the lines $x = 1, x = 4$.

8 The diagram shows part of the curve with equation $y = \dfrac{1}{x^2}$. Find the value of k for which area A has the same value as area B.

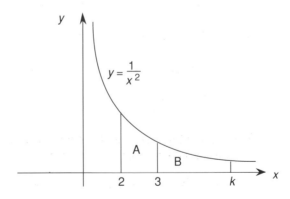

SUMMARY   We have seen in this section how integration is the reverse of differentiation and we have found the integral of simple functions of x. Be careful to include the constant C when you present your answer and make sure you understand when integrating what algebraic methods can be legitimately applied.

10

Numerical methods

This short section deals with two topics from a large and useful section of maths: numerical methods. In the real world, there are fewer integers and equations which work out nicely: a whole array of techniques has been evolved to work out approximations to the resulting problems. We shall see how we can improve accuracy in using arithmetic operations and how we can start the process of finding roots for equations with no exact solutions.

Errors

The solutions to questions are often asked for 'correct to 1 decimal place': suppose we are answering such a question and the final line of our working is:

$$x = 5.2 \times 3.3 \quad = \quad 17.16$$
$$= \quad 17.2 \text{ (1 d.p.)}$$

How accurate is the solution? Can we really be sure about that last decimal place?

To see this, we have to look at the figures used to work out the value for x, i.e. 5.2 and 3.3. If those figures themselves are correct to one decimal place, then 5.2 could have started as anything between 5.15 and 5.25, while 3.3 could have been anything between 3.25 and 3.35, before rounding. So the least possible value of the product is:

$$5.15 \times 3.25 \quad = \quad 16.74 \quad = \quad 16.7 \quad \text{(1 d.p.)}$$

and the greatest possible value is:

$$5.25 \times 3.35 \quad = \quad 17.59 \quad = \quad 17.6 \quad \text{(1 d.p.)}$$

The answer to the question about the accuracy of the solution is – not very accurate! We certainly couldn't say for sure what the decimal place was: in fact we couldn't even say for sure whether the answer was 17 or 18 to the nearest whole number.

This is why, when asked to give a solution correct to a certain number of decimal places, you should work throughout to an *extra two decimal places*, only rounding off to give the final solution. In this way, the solution is very probably correct to the required number of decimal places.

Maximum and minimum values

In order to find out the maximum or minimum possible value for some combinations of figures that have been rounded off to a certain number of decimal places, we can always use the method above, whereby we combine all the upper limits to give the maximum and the lower limits for the minimum. For example, if we wanted to find the maximum value for 5.2 + 3.3, we would say that the value of 5.2 could be as much as 5.25 and that of 3.3 could be 3.35. Then the sum could be as much as 5.25 + 3.35 = 8.6.

We have to be a little careful sometimes in working out the separate values of the terms which give an overall maximum. To find the greatest value of 5.2 − 3.3, for instance, we would not take the same limits as for the sum, i.e. 5.25 and 3.35, but rather the maximum value for the 5.2 and the *minimum* value for the 3.3, i.e. 3.25, giving overall 5.25 − 3.25 = 2.0 as the maximum value. Similarly for division: if we want the maximum value of $\frac{5.2}{3.3}$, we take $\frac{5.25}{3.25}$ which gives 1.62, and for the minimum, $\frac{5.15}{3.35}$ to give 1.54.

Absolute and relative errors

When figures are given correct to 1 d.p., as were 5.2 and 3.3 in the last example, the error could be up to 0.05 either way in each case. This error, due to the rounding up or down, is called an *absolute* error of *magnitude* 0.05 (i.e. the size is 0.05, but it could be positive or negative). An absolute error of 0.05 is probably not very serious in a quantity of size 2000. In a quantity of size 0.2, the same error of 0.05 is very much more serious, representing a 25% error either way. To give an idea of the relative size of the error and the quantity, we define the *relative error* to be:

$$\frac{\text{error}}{\text{quantity}} = \text{relative error}$$

This is frequently multiplied by 100% to give the *percentage relative error*.

Then, according to the operations we're performing on the approximate quantities, there are two distinct formulae ...

adding or subtracting: add | absolute errors |

and the other is:

> multiplying or dividing: add relative errors

So if we were adding or subtracting the 5.2 and 3.3, both of which are subject to an absolute error of magnitude 0.05, the sum or difference is subject to an absolute error of magnitude 0.05 + 0.05 = 0.1. Since 5.2 + 3.3 = 8.5, we can say that the answer is 8.5 ± 0.1.

In multiplying or dividing the same two numbers, the *absolute* error in 5.2 is a *relative* error of $\frac{0.05}{5.2} \approx 0.01 = 1\%$ (the wavy equals sign means 'approximately equal to'), and the absolute error in 3.3 is a relative error of $\frac{0.05}{3.3} \approx 1.5\%$. Using the formula of adding relative errors, we can expect a relative error in the product of about 2.5%, i.e. 17.16 ± 0.43 which you can see agrees quite closely with the limits we worked out before.

You should now be able to answer Exercises 1, 2 and 3 on page 134.

Location of roots

A *root* of an equation $f(x) = 0$ is the value of x which makes the equation true. $x^2 - 4 = 0$, for example, has the two roots $x = 2$ and $x = -2$. Most equations which occur naturally have no *exact* solution: the best we can do is to find a first approximation to a solution and then, using various methods, improve the accuracy to the required degree.

We can use a variety of approaches to find this first approximation: algebraic methods will work for linear, quadratic and some other polynomial equations, while a geometric method, finding the intersection of graphs, may be easier to use in other cases.

Using this latter approach, if we can write the equation we're trying to solve in the form $f(x) = 0$, the *root* (possibly more than one) is the point at which the graph of $y = f(x)$ crosses the line $y = 0$ (i.e. the *x*-axis).

Figure 10.1

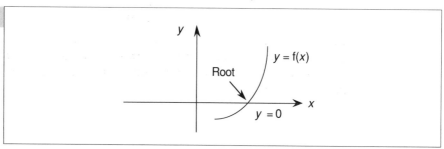

As you can see from Figure 10.1, if the graph crosses the x-axis with a positive gradient, then just before the root $f(x)$ is negative and just after $f(x)$ is positive. With a negative gradient the opposite would be true.

This fact forms the basis for a method of finding the first approximation to a root. We try different values of x in the function $f(x)$: we're not expecting a value of x which makes $f(x)$ zero (since this would be an exact root); rather, we're looking for a change of sign in $f(x)$.

Suppose for example that for the function of $f(x)$ sketched above we found that $f(2) = -2$ and $f(3) = 4$. We can say that there was a root in the interval $2 < x < 3$. This is the first stage in finding an approximate numerical value to the root – finding an interval for x in which it lies.

Let's see how the method works for a straightforward algebraic equation:

$$f(x) \quad = \quad x^3 - x - 12 = 0$$

We'll put in some values for x:

$$f(0) \quad = \quad -12$$
$$f(1) \quad = \quad -12$$
$$f(2) \quad = \quad -6$$
$$f(3) \quad = \quad 12$$

and we can see that there is a root between 2 and 3. Here's a sketch of part of the graph of the function:

Figure 10.2

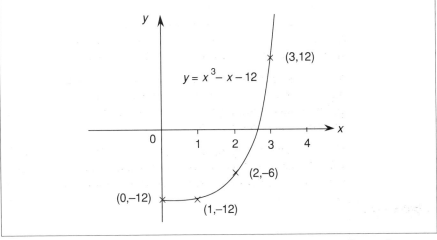

One thing you must remember with this method is to use *radians* whenever the function involves any trigonometric function. Let's have a look at an example of this:

Example	By finding values of f(x) for $x = 0$, 1 and 2, where

$$f(x) \quad = \quad e^x - 10 \cos x$$

locate an approximate root for the equation f(x) = 0

Solution	In radians!

$$f(0) \quad = \quad 1 - 10 \quad = \quad -9$$
$$f(1) \quad = \quad 2.7 - 5.4 \quad = \quad -2.7$$
$$f(2) \quad = \quad 7.4 + 4.1 \quad = \quad 11.5$$

Since there is a change in sign between f(1) and f(2), there is a root for some value of x in the range:

$$1 < x < 2$$

You should now be able to complete Exercises 4, 5 and 6 on pp. 134–135.

EXERCISES

1 If A = 3.7 and B = 7.2, both of these correct to one decimal place, give the maximum and minimum values of:

   a   A + B

   b   B − A

   c   A × B

   d   B ÷ A

2 If the absolute errors in p and q have a maximum magnitude of 0.05, find the maximum magnitude of the absolute error in:

   a $p + q$

   b $3p + 2q$

   c $3p - 2q$

3 If the maximum relative errors in s and t are both 0.5%, find the maximum relative error in:

   a s^2

   b st

   c $\dfrac{s^2}{t}$

4 By finding the value of f(x) for different values of x, deduce approximate roots for the equations f(x) = 0 when:

   a $f(x) = x^3 - 8x - 4 \qquad (x > 0)$

b $f(x) = \ln x + x - 4$ $(x > 0)$

c $f(x) = e^x + x - 8$

d $f(x) = 2 \sin x + x - 3$ (use radians)

5 Show that the equation $e^x \cos 2x - 1 = 0$ has a root between 0.4 and 0.45 (use radians).

6 Show that the equation: $(x + 1)^5 = (x + 2)^3 + 4$

has a root between 0.8 and 1.

[Take all terms to one side, so that you're left with $f(x) = 0$.]

SUMMARY   When you have finished this section, you should be a little more aware of the dangers involved in calculations where the numbers are rounded off too early. You should also appreciate that the root of an equation of the form $f(x) = 0$ occurs between a positive and a negative value of the function $f(x)$, and use this fact to give a region within which the root lies.

MODULE

P1

Solutions

Section 1

1 **a** $3x^3 + 3x^2 + 6x - 12$ **b** $2x^3 + x^2 + 6x - 16$

  c $x^3 - 5x^2 + 8x - 10$ **d** $x^3 + 2x^2 + 4$

2 **a** $x^2 + 10x + 9$ **b** $x^2 + 8x + 15$

  c $x^2 + x - 12$ **d** $x^2 + 4x - 12$

  e $x^2 - 5x + 6$ **f** $x^2 - 6x + 5$

  g $2x^2 + 3x + 1$ **h** $3x^2 + 8x + 4$

  i $3x^2 + 2x - 1$ **j** $4x^2 - 1$

  k $6x^2 - 11x + 3$ **l** $8x^2 - 6x - 9$

3 **a** $1 + 3x - 17x^2 + 14x^3$

  b $6 - 11x + 11x^2 + 2x^3 - 8x^4$

4 **a** $\dfrac{2x+5}{(x+2)(x+3)}$ **b** $\dfrac{x+5}{(x+3)(x+4)}$

  c $\dfrac{1}{(x-5)(x-4)}$ **d** $\dfrac{8x}{x^2-4}$

  e $\dfrac{5x-9}{(x-3)^2}$ **f** $\dfrac{5x+9}{x^2-9}$

5 **a** $(x+2)(x+3)$ **b** $(x+4)(x-2)$

  c $(x-5)(x+4)$ **d** $(x-5)(x-6)$

  e $(a-5)(a-2)$ **f** $(b+6)(b+4)$

  g $(y-5)(y-4)$ **h** $(p-9)(p+2)$

  i $x(x+3)(x-2)$ **j** $x(x+8)(x-5)$

6 **a** $(3x-1)(x-5)$ **b** $(2x+1)(x-3)$

  c $(5x-7)(x+1)$ **d** $(3x-2)(2x-3)$

7 **a** $x^2 + 4x + 4$ **b** $x^2 - 8x + 16$

  c $x^2 + x + \dfrac{1}{4}$ **d** $x^2 + \dfrac{4x}{3} + \dfrac{4}{9}$

  e $4x^2 + 4x + 1$ **f** $9x^2 + 30x + 25$

  g $4x^2 - 28x + 49$ **h** $x^2 + 2ax + a^2$

  i $b^2x^2 + 2bcx + c^2$ **j** $p^2x^2 - 2pqx + q^2$

8 **a** $(x+1)^2 + 3$ **b** $(x+4)^2 - 20$

  c $(x-2)^2 - 3$ **d** $(x-5)^2 - 5$

  e $(x+2)(x-1) - 1$ **f** $(x-2)(x-1) - 7$

9 **a** $2\left[(x-2)^2 - \dfrac{3}{2}\right] = 2(x-2)^2 - 3$

  b $3\left[\left(x + \dfrac{5}{3}\right)^2 - \dfrac{16}{9}\right]$

  c $24 - (x+4)^2$

  d $2\left[\dfrac{73}{16} - \left(x - \dfrac{5}{4}\right)^2\right]$

137

Section 2

1 $g(2) = 2^2 + 2 = 6$, $g(5) = 27$, $g(0) = 2$, $g(-1) = 3$

2 **a** $p: x \longmapsto 4x + 3$ or $p(x) = 4x + 3$

  b $q: x \longmapsto \dfrac{x}{2} - 2$ or $q(x) = \dfrac{x}{2} - 2$

  c $r: x \longmapsto 2\sqrt{x}$ or $r(x) = 2\sqrt{x}$

3 $p(2) = 11$, $p(-4) = -13$, $q(4) = 0$, $q(-8) = -6$,
  $r(100) = 20$, $r(0) = 0$

4 **a** No restrictions

  b x must be positive for the domain *and* range

  c No restriction on domain, but range is
  limited to numbers greater than or equal to -3

  d No restriction on domain, range is numbers
  less than or equal to 1

5 p is 1–1, q is 1–1, r is 1–1, k is 1–1, l is 1–1, s is
  many – 1, t is many – 1

6 $g^{-1}: x \longmapsto \dfrac{x+3}{2}$

  $h^{-1}: x \longmapsto \sqrt[3]{x}$

  $k^{-1}: x \longmapsto \dfrac{1-x}{x}$, $x \neq 0$

  $l^{-1}: x \longmapsto \dfrac{3x-1}{x-2}$, $x \neq 2$

7 $f^{-1}: x \longmapsto \dfrac{x}{2}$

  $fg: x \longmapsto 2x + 4$

  $gf: x \longmapsto 2x + 2$

  $fh: x \longmapsto \dfrac{2}{x}$

  $gh: x \longmapsto \dfrac{1}{x} + 2$

  $\dfrac{x}{2} = \dfrac{2}{x} \Rightarrow x^2 = 4$ and $x = \pm 2$

8 $fg: x \longmapsto 3x^2 + 22$

  $gf: x \longmapsto 9x^2 + 24x + 22$

9 $gf(x) = g\left[\dfrac{x-1}{x+2}\right]$

  $= \dfrac{1-2\left(\dfrac{x-1}{x+2}\right)}{1-\left(\dfrac{x-1}{x+2}\right)}$

$= \dfrac{(x+2)-2x+2}{(x+2)-x+1} = \dfrac{4-x}{3}$

10 $g^2(x) = g\left(\dfrac{1-2x}{1-x}\right)$

  $= \dfrac{1-2\left(\dfrac{1-2x}{1-x}\right)}{1-\left(\dfrac{1-2x}{1-x}\right)}$

  $= \dfrac{(1-x)-2+4x}{(1-x)-1+2x} = \dfrac{3x-1}{x}$

11 **a** Odd **b** Even **c** Neither **d** Even
  e Neither **f** Even **g** Neither **h** Even
  i Odd **j** Odd

12 **a**

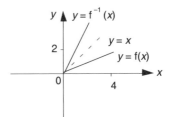

  b

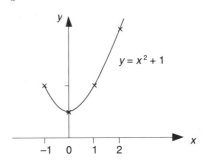

No inverse, because there is a turning-point
when $x = 0$

  c

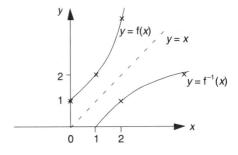

13

a

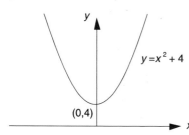

$y = x^2 + 4$

(0,4)

b

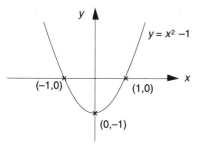

$y = x^2 - 1$

(−1,0)   (1,0)

(0,−1)

c

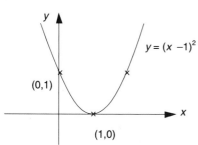

$y = (x - 1)^2$

(0,1)

(1,0)

d

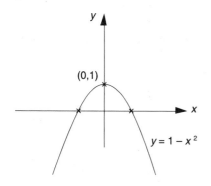

(0,1)

$y = 1 - x^2$

14

a

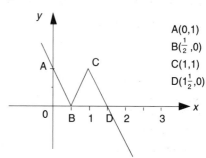

A(0,1)
B($\frac{1}{2}$,0)
C(1,1)
D($1\frac{1}{2}$,0)

b

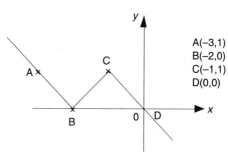

A(−3,1)
B(−2,0)
C(−1,1)
D(0,0)

Section 3

1 **a** 5 **b** 13 **c** 10

2 **a** $-\dfrac{4}{3}$ **b** $-\dfrac{12}{5}$ **c** $-\dfrac{4}{3}$

3 **a** 2,–3 **b** 1,4

4 **a** $y = 5x - 2$ **b** $y = x$ **c** $y + 3x = 1$
   d $2y + x = 4$

5 **a** $y = 3x - 5$ **b** $2y = x + 6$
   c $y = 2x$ **d** $5y = 3x + 13$

6

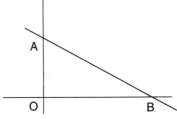

The line has gradient $\dfrac{3-1}{2-6} = -\dfrac{1}{2}$, so equation is

$y = -\dfrac{1}{2}x + c$

Putting in (6,1) $1 = -3 + c \Rightarrow c = 4$

Equation is $y = -\dfrac{1}{2}x + 4 \Rightarrow 2y = -x + 8$

When $x = 0$, $y = 4 \Rightarrow OA = 4$

$y = 0$, $x = 8 \Rightarrow OB = 8$

Area Δ is $\dfrac{1}{2}$ base $\times$ height $= \dfrac{1}{2} \times 8 \times 4 = 16$

7 **a** (1,4) **b** (4,3)

8 **a**

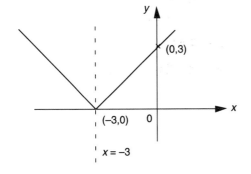

b

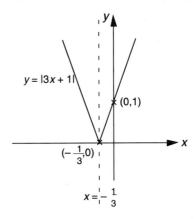

c

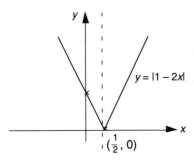

Section 4

1 a 2 **b** –3 **c** –22

2 a $a = 3$ **b** $x = 3$
  $y = 4$ $y = 2$

3 a $x = 2$
  $y = 3$
  b $x = -3$
  $y = -7$
  c $x = -2$
  $y = -3$

4 a $x = 3$ or $x = 4$ **b** $x = 4$ or $x = -3$
  c $x = \dfrac{2}{3}$ or $x = -4$

5 a $x = 7$ or $x = -5$ **b** $x = -3$ or $x = 8$
  c $x = -\dfrac{3}{2} \pm \dfrac{\sqrt{15}}{2}$

6 a 0.13, –1.88 **b** 3.85, 0.65 **c** 0.23, –2.90

7 We are given that the length $L = 100$ and the sag $y = 10$. Substituting these values,

$$100 = x + \frac{800}{3x}$$

multiply throughout the equation by $3x$

$$300x = 3x^2 + 800$$

$$\Rightarrow 3x^2 - 300x + 800 = 0$$

Use the formula for this,

$$x = \frac{300 \pm \sqrt{90{,}000 - 9600}}{6}$$

$$= \frac{300 \pm 283.55}{6}$$

Taking the negative value gives a value of x which is too small. Taking the positive,

$$x = \frac{300 + 283.55}{6} = 97.3 \text{ m}$$

8 a Even though taking the y involves fractions, we'll take this because we only have to substitute once:

$$3y = 1 - x \quad \Rightarrow \frac{1-x}{3}$$

$$x^2 + 3x + 5\left(\frac{1-x}{3}\right) = 20 \qquad \text{multiply by 3}$$

$$3x^2 + 9x + 5(1 - x) = 20$$

$$3x^2 + 9x + 5 - 5x = 20$$

$$3x^2 + 4x - 15 = 0$$

$$(3x - 5)(x + 3) = 0$$

$$x = \frac{5}{3} \qquad x = -3$$

and $\quad y = -\dfrac{2}{9} \quad y = \dfrac{4}{3}$

b Take the x here, because $(2x)^2$ is exactly $4x^2$

$$2x = 8 - y \Rightarrow (2x)^2 = 4x^2 = (8 - y)^2$$

$$(8 - y)^2 + 3y^2 = 52$$

$$\Rightarrow 64 - 16y + y^2 + 3y^2 = 52$$

$$4y^2 - 16y + 12 = 0$$

$$y^2 - 4y + 3 = 0$$

$$(y - 3)(y - 1) = 0$$

$$y = 3 \qquad \text{or} \qquad y = 1$$

$$x = \frac{5}{2} \qquad \text{or} \qquad x = \frac{7}{2}$$

c Take the y for both the preceding reasons!

$$2y = 5 - x \Rightarrow 4y^2 = (5 - x)^2 = 25 - 10x + x^2$$

$$5x^2 + (25 - 10x + x^2) + 12x = 29$$

$$6x^2 + 2x - 4 = 0$$

$$(6x - 4)(x + 1) = 0 \quad x = \frac{2}{3} \qquad x = -1$$

$$y = \frac{13}{6} \qquad y = 3$$

9 a $x < 4$
  b $x > -6$

10 a $-4 < x < 4$
  b $x \le -\sqrt{5}$ or $x \ge \sqrt{5}$
  c $x < 5$ or $x > -1$
  d $x \ge \dfrac{1}{3}$ or $x \le -1$
  e $-2 < x < 5$
  f $x < -4$ or $x > 3$
  g $x > 3$ or $x < -\dfrac{1}{2}$
  h $x > 3 + \sqrt{10}$ or $x < 3 - \sqrt{10}$

Section 5

1   **a** 1 **b** 1 **c** 1/2 **d** 1/9 **e** 0.001
    f 4 **g** 8 **h** 32 **i** 3 **j** x^{-5}

2   **a** 5 **b** 4 **c** 1/2 **d** 9 **e** 32 **f** 4 **g** 8

3   **a** $10\sqrt{3}$ **b** $5\sqrt{3}$ **c** $4\sqrt{2}$ **d** $2\sqrt{2}$ **e** $7\sqrt{2}$
    f $4\sqrt{3}$

4   **a** $2\sqrt{5}$ **b** $3\sqrt{7}$ **c** $5(3-2\sqrt{2}) = 15 - 10\sqrt{2}$
    d $4(\sqrt{14}+ 2\sqrt{3}) = 4\sqrt{14} + 8\sqrt{3}$

5

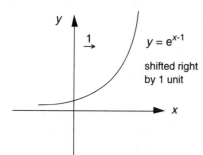

a

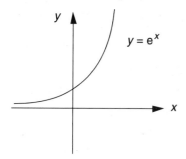

shifted right
by 1 unit

b

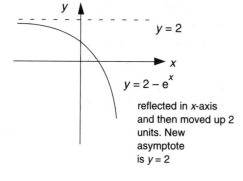

reflected in *x*-axis
and then moved up 2
units. New
asymptote
is $y = 2$

6

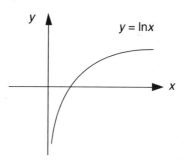

a

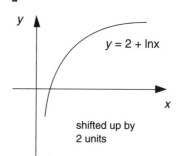

shifted up by
2 units

b

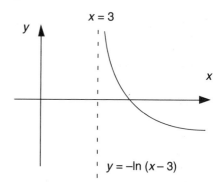

Shifted right by 3, then reflected in *x*-axis.
New asymptote at $x = 3$.

Section 6

1 **a** $u_{n+1} = u_n + 3 : u_1 = 1$

   b $u_{n+1} = 2u_n : u_1 = 1$

   c $u_{n+1} = u_n + (2n + 1) : u_1 = 2$

2 **a** $u_r = 3r - 2$

   b $u_r = 2^{r-1}$

   c $u_r = r^2 + 1$

3 **a** periodic

   b divergent

   c convergent

   d oscillating

   e convergent

   f oscillating and periodic

4 **a** oscillates between $0 - 1$

   b diverges

   c oscillates between $0 - 1$

   d diverges

   e oscillates between $0 - 1$

5 **a** The rule here is 'double r and add 1', so the 10th term is 21 and in general, the rth term is $2r + 1$.

   b The rule is 'multiply r by 3', so the 10th term is 30 and r^{th} term is $3r$.

   c The rule is 'multiply r by 4 and subtract 3', so 10th term is 37 and r^{th} term is $4r - 3$.

6 **c** $\displaystyle\sum_{r=1}^{15} (2r + 1)$

   b $\displaystyle\sum_{r=1}^{33} 3r$

   c $\displaystyle\sum_{r=1}^{26} (4r - 3)$

7 **a** First three terms are   7, 11, 15

      Last two terms are   59, 63

   b First three terms are   3, 1, –1

      Last two terms are   –15, –17

   c First three terms are   4, 9, 16

      Last two terms are   361, 400

8 **a** 3, 4, 5, 6, 7

      u_{10}, the 10th term, is $3 + 9(1) \;=\; 12$

      Sum of the first 16 terms, S_{16}, is

$$\tfrac{16}{2}\left\{2(3) + (16 - 1)\,1\right\}$$

$$= \quad 8\{6 + 15\} = 168$$

   b –2, 1, 4, 7, 10

$$u_{10} = -2 + 9(3) = 25$$

$$S_{16} = \tfrac{16}{2}\left\{2(-2) + 15(3)\right\}$$

$$= \quad 8\left\{41\right\} = 328$$

   c 100, 96, 92, 88, 84

$$u_{10} = 100 + 9\,(-4) = 64$$

$$S_{16} = \tfrac{16}{2}\{200 + 15\,(-4)\}$$

$$= \quad 8\{140\} = 1120$$

9 Here we have to calculate u_{20} and S_{20}: we can find S_{20} most conveniently by the formula $S_n = \tfrac{n}{2}\{$first + last $\}$, since 'last' means u_{20} which we've already calculated.

   a $a = 1$ and $d = 4.$ $u_{20} = 1 + 19\,(4) = 77.$

$$S_{20} = \tfrac{20}{2}\left\{1 + 77\right\} = 780$$

   b $a = 2$ and $d = 0.2.$ $u_{20} = 2 + 19\,(0.2) = 5.8$

$$S_{20} = \tfrac{20}{2}\left\{2 + 5.8\right\} \quad = 78$$

   c $a = 240$ and $d = -20.$

$$u_{20} = 240 + 19\,(-20) = -140$$

$$S_{20} = \tfrac{20}{2}\left\{240 - 140\right\} = 1000$$

10 Given that (i) $S_{10} = 20$ and (ii) $S_{20} = 10$

   a $(S_{10} =) \tfrac{10}{2}\left\{2a + 9d\right\} = 20$ and

   b $(S_{20} =) \tfrac{20}{2}\left\{2a + 19d\right\} = 10$

      i.e. (i) $2a + 9d = 4$ ...... [1]

      and (ii) $2a + 19d = 1$ ...... [2]

      Subtracting, $10d = -3$, i.e. $d = -0.3$

      and $a = 3.35$

    Then $S_{40} = \tfrac{40}{2}\left\{6.7 + 39\,(-0.3)\right\}$

$$= \quad 20(-5) = \quad -100$$

11 Series is $p + q,\ 2p + q,\ 3p + q,\ ...$

$$U_6 = 4U_2 \Rightarrow \quad 6p + q = 4\,(2p + q)$$

$$\Rightarrow \quad 2p + 3q = 0 \quad [1]$$

$$S_3 = 12 \Rightarrow \quad 6p + 3q = 12 \quad [2]$$

    Solve [1] and [2] simultaneously to give

    $p = 3$ and $q = -2.$

12 $8, 4, 2, 1, \frac{1}{2}$

$$u_{10} = 8 \times \left(\frac{1}{2}\right)^9 = \frac{1}{64}$$

$$S_{10} = \frac{8\left(1-\left(\frac{1}{2}\right)^{10}\right)}{\frac{1}{2}} = 16 - \frac{16}{2^{10}} = 16 - \frac{1}{64}$$

$$S_{\infty} = \frac{8}{1-\frac{1}{2}} = 16$$

13   Geometric series, $a = 1.1$ and $r = 1.1$

$$S_{20} = \frac{1.1(1-1.1^{20})}{1-1.1} = 11(5.7275)$$

$$= 63 \quad \text{(to two significant figures)}$$

14   Split this into two series,

$$\sum_{r=1}^{10} r + \sum_{r=1}^{10} 2^r, \text{ first arithmetic, sum } \frac{10(11)}{2} = 55$$

and second geometric, sum $\frac{2(2^{10}-1)}{2-1} = 2046$. So

total is 2101.

15   Suppose the smaller is a, and the common ratio r, then the four children receive

a, ar, ar^2, ar^3

From information given,

$a + ar + ar^2 + ar^3 = \quad 1005 \quad [1]$

and $\quad\quad ar^3 = \quad 8a \quad\quad [2]$

From [2], $r = 2$ and putting this into [1] gives

$15a = \quad 1005$

$a = \quad 67$

The amounts allocated are then 67, 134, 268, 536 respectively.

16   Since the maximum speeds form a geometric series, we can write them as a, ar, ar^2 and ar^3, And take $a = 20$ and $ar^3 = 200$. Dividing these gives $r^3 = 10 \Rightarrow r = 2.154$

So the maximum speed in second gear, ar, will be $20 \times 2.154 = 43.1$ kmh^{-1} and the maximum in third, ar^2, will be $20 \times 2.154^2 = 92.8$ kmh^{-1}.

17   **a**   An increment of 8% means that the estimated salary at the beginning of a new year will be the previous salary multiplied by a factor of $1 + 8\% = 1.08$.

For 1993, her estimated salary will be

£7000 × 1.08 = £7560

and in 1994, £7560 × 1.8 = £8164.80

b   The total earned will be a GP, with $a = £7000$ and $r = 1.08$.
After n complete years, this will be

$$\frac{a(r^n-1)}{r-1} = £ \frac{7000(1.08^n-1)}{1.08-1}$$

i.e. £S = £87500 $(1.08^n - 1)$

when $n = 10$, S = 87500 $(1.08^{10} - 1) = £101,400$ (nearest £100)

18   For an arithmetic progression, if a, b and c are consecutive terms,

$b - a = c - b$

i.e. $x^2 - 1 = x - x^2$

$2x^2 - x - 1 = 0$

$(2x + 1)(x - 1) = 0$

i.e. $x = -\frac{1}{2}$ or $x = 1$

19   From the information,

a $\frac{x}{1} = \frac{y}{x}$ and **b** $x - 1 = -y - x$

a $x^2 = y$ [1]

b $y = 1 - 2x$ [2]

Putting [1] into [2] gives $x^2 = 1 - 2x$,

i.e. $x^2 + 2x - 1 = 0$

Using the quadratic formula,

$$x = \frac{-2\pm\sqrt{(4+4)}}{2}$$

$$= \frac{-2\pm\sqrt{8}}{2} = -1 \pm \sqrt{2}$$

x is positive, so x must be $-1 + \sqrt{2}$

Then $\quad y \quad = x^2$

$= (-1 + \sqrt{2})^2 = 1 - 2\sqrt{2} + 2$

$= 3 - 2\sqrt{2}$

20   Since the number of terms is very small here, it's easier to use the actual terms rather than the formula.

First three terms are $1, r, r^2$ and then, from given information,

$1 + r + r^2 \quad = 7r^2$

i.e. $6r^2 - r - 1 \quad = \quad 0$

$(3r + 1)(2r - 1) \quad = \quad 0$

$\therefore \quad r = -\frac{1}{3}$ or $r = \quad \frac{1}{2}$

In both cases there is a sum to infinity, since the modulus of r is less than 1.

$$r = -\frac{1}{3} \Rightarrow S_\infty = \frac{1}{1-r} = \frac{1}{1+\frac{1}{3}} = \frac{3}{4}$$

and $\quad r = \frac{1}{2} \Rightarrow S_\infty = \frac{a}{1-r} = \frac{1}{1-\frac{1}{2}} = 2$

Section 7

1 **a** 2π **b** $\dfrac{\pi}{3}$ **c** $\dfrac{3\pi}{2}$ **d** 3π **e** $\dfrac{5\pi}{6}$

  f $\dfrac{\pi}{12}$ **g** $\dfrac{5\pi}{12}$ **h** $\dfrac{5\pi}{4}$ **i** $\dfrac{7\pi}{4}$ **j** $\dfrac{3\pi}{4}$

2 **a** 60° **b** 135° **c** 120° **d** 150° **e** 270°

  f 720° **g** 225° **h** 210° **i** 300° **j** 18°

3 **a** Whole circumference is $2\pi r = 8\pi$, segment is $\dfrac{90}{360} \times 8\pi = 2\pi$ cm

  Whole area is $\pi r^2 = 16\pi$, segment is 4π cm²

  b 14π cm, 84π cm²

  c 6π, 24π cm²

  d 15π, 67.5π cm²

4 **a** graph of $y = \sin x$ shifted down 2, so range is $-1 < y < -3$

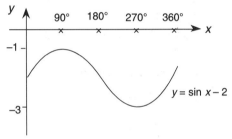

  b graph of $y = \cos x$ shifted back 60°

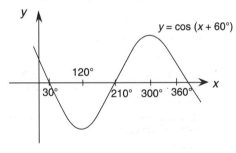

c graph of $y = \tan x$ shifted forwards by 45°

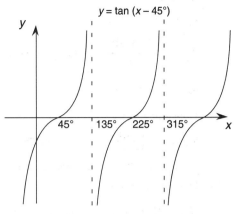

  d graph of $y = \cos x$ shifted forwards by 30°, scaling y-direction factor 2

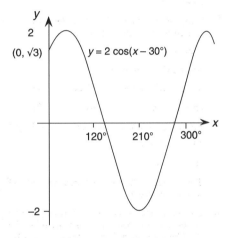

  e graph of $y = \cos x$ reflected in x-axis

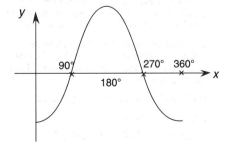

5 **a**   330°, 570°, 690°

  b   36.9°, 323.1°, 396.9°, 683.1°

  c   76.0°, 256.0°, 436.0°, 616.0°

6 **a**   0.93, $\pi - 0.93 = 2.21$

  b   1.16, $2\pi - 1.16 = 5.12$

  c   (One angle is −1.19)
       $\pi - 1.19 = 1.95$
       $2\pi - 1.19 = 5.09$

7 **a**   53.1°, 126.9°

  b   −66.4°, 66.4°

  c   −87.7°, 92.3°

8 **a**   8.7°, 81.3°, 188.7°, 261.3°

  b   60°, 120°, 240°, 300°

  c   67.5°, 157.5°, 247.5°, 337.5°

9 $x - 10° = \pm 60° \Rightarrow x = 70°$ or $-50°$

10 $2\theta + \dfrac{\pi}{4} = \dfrac{3\pi}{4}$ or $\dfrac{7\pi}{4}$

   $\Rightarrow 2\theta = \dfrac{\pi}{2}$ or $\dfrac{3\pi}{2}$

   $\Rightarrow \theta = \dfrac{\pi}{4}$ or $\dfrac{3\pi}{4}$

Section 8

1 a $\dfrac{(2.01)^2-2^2}{(2.01)-2} = \dfrac{4.0401-4}{0.01}$

$= 4.01$

b $\dfrac{(2.001)^2-2^2}{2.001-2} = \dfrac{4.004001-4}{0.001}$

$= 4.001$

c $\dfrac{(2.0000001)^2-2^2}{2.0000001-2}$

$= \dfrac{4.00000040000001}{0.0000001} - 4$

$= 4.0000001$

2 a $6x$ **b** $16x^3$ **c** $1-\dfrac{1}{x^2}$ **d** $\dfrac{1}{4}x^{-3/4}$

e $\dfrac{1}{5}x^{-4/5} - \dfrac{5}{2}x^{-3/2}$ **f** $\dfrac{5}{2}x^{3/2}$ **g** $-\dfrac{1}{3}x^{-4/3}$

h $\dfrac{-20}{x^5}$ **i** $-3x^{-7/4}$ **j** $2x-\dfrac{2}{x^3}$

3 a $\dfrac{dy}{dx} = 12x^2 = 12$ when $x = 1$

b $\dfrac{dy}{dx} = 4x - 1 = 7$ when $x = 2$

c $\dfrac{dy}{dx} = 2x - \dfrac{2}{x^3} = 0$ when $x = 1$

d $\dfrac{dy}{dx} = \dfrac{3}{2}x^{1/2} + \dfrac{3}{2}x^{-5/2} = 3\dfrac{3}{64}$ when $x = 4$

e $\dfrac{dy}{dx} = 2x + 4 = 4$ when $x = 0$

4 a We could of course 'complete the square' to find the turning point:

$y = x^2 - 2x + 5 = (x-1)^2 + 4$

so a minimum value (since the coefficient of x^2 is positive) of 4 when $x = 1$, i.e. the point $(1, 4)$.

Anyway, using the calculus,

$\dfrac{dy}{dx} = 2x - 2 = 0$ for turning point(s)

Then $x = 1$, giving $y = 4$:

$\dfrac{d^2y}{dx^2} = 2$; positive

So $(1, 4)$ is a minimum point.

b $y = 12x - x^3$

$\dfrac{dy}{dx} = 12 - 3x^2 = 0$ for turning points

Then $3x^2 = 12$, $x^2 = 4$, $x = \pm 2$. Two turning points, but let's find $\dfrac{d^2y}{dx^2}$ first.

$\dfrac{d^2y}{dx^2} = -6x$

a $x = 2$, giving $y = 16$ and $\dfrac{d^2y}{dx^2} = -12$; negative

So $(2, 16)$ is a maximum point.

b $x = -2$, giving $y = -16$ and $\dfrac{d^2y}{dx^2} = 12$, positive

So $(-2, -16)$ is a minimum point.

5 a $\dfrac{3}{x}$ **b** $\dfrac{1}{x} - e^x$ **c** $4e^{4x}$ **d** $6e^{2x}$ **e** $\dfrac{-1}{x^2} + \dfrac{1}{x}$

6 Differentiating both sides of the given equation with respect to V,

$\dfrac{dC}{dV} = -\dfrac{16000}{V^2} + 2V$ [1]

For a stationary point, $\dfrac{dC}{dV} = 0$

$\Rightarrow -\dfrac{16000}{V^2} + 2V = 0$

$\Rightarrow 2V^3 - 16000 = 0$

$\Rightarrow V^3 = 8000$

$\Rightarrow V = 20$

Differentiating [1] again gives $\dfrac{d^2C}{dV^2} = \dfrac{32000}{V^3} + 2$

We don't need to substitute the value of V to see that this must be *positive* and so the value of V gives a minimum value for C.

7

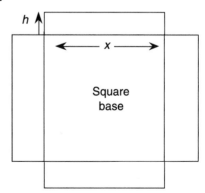

Let the height be h, so that the volume is cross-sectional area × height, i.e.

$V = x^2h$ [1]

Area of sheet used is $x^2 + 4 \times xh$, i.e.

  Base Side

$A = x^2 + 4xh$ [2]

Rearranging [1] gives $h = \dfrac{V}{x^2}$, and putting this in [2] gives:

$$A = x^2 + \dfrac{4xV}{x^2} = x^2 + \dfrac{4V}{x}$$

which is the expression required.

Differentiating this with respect to x:

$$\dfrac{dA}{dx} = 2x - \dfrac{4V}{x^2} = 0 \quad \text{for turning point(s)}$$

i.e.: $\quad 2x^3 = 4V$

$$V = \dfrac{x^3}{2}$$

Putting this into [1] gives: $\dfrac{x^3}{2} = x^2 h$

$x = 2h$

$x : h = 2 : 1$ which is the required ratio for a minimum area.

(It *is* a minimum since $\dfrac{d^2A}{dx^2} = 2 + \dfrac{8V}{x^3} > 0$.)

8   Two pieces of the wire are $x + x + x + x = 4x$ cm in length each. The other piece is $y + x + y + x = 2y + 2x$. In total the length is $2y + 6x$.

Given that this is 450, we can write the equation

$2y + 6x = 450$ $\hspace{3em}$ [1]

The volume is $x \times x \times y = x^2 y = V$ $\hspace{1em}$ [2]

From [1]. $2y = 450 - 6x \Rightarrow y = 225{-}3x$ $\hspace{1em}$ [3]

Put [3] into [2], $V = x^2 y = x^2 (225{-}3x)$

i.e. $\quad V = 225x^2 - 3x^3$ $\hspace{2em}$ [4]

Now we have this in terms of just one variable, we differentiate,

$$\dfrac{dV}{dx} = 450x - 9x^2 \hspace{4em} [5]$$

For a turning point, $\dfrac{dV}{dx} = 0 \Rightarrow 450x - 9x^2 = 0$

$$9x\,(50 - x) = 0$$

$$\Rightarrow \quad x = 0 \ \text{or} \ x = 50$$

Putting this value into [3], $y = 225{-}150 = 75$

Differentiating [5], $\dfrac{d^2V}{dx^2} = 450{-}18x$

When $x = 50$, $\dfrac{d^2V}{dx^2} = 450{-}900 = -450 < 0$

The values of x and y give a *maximum* volume.

Section 9

1 **a** $4x^3$ and $\dfrac{x^4}{4}$

b $8x^7$ and $\dfrac{x^8}{8}$

c $-2x^{-3}$ and $-\dfrac{1}{2}x^{-2}$

d 4 and $5x$

2 **a** $x^4 + C$ **b** $\dfrac{2}{5}x^5 + C$

c $-\dfrac{1}{3}x^{-3} + C$ (or $\dfrac{-1}{3x^3} + C$)

d $\dfrac{-5}{2}x^{-2} + C$ (or $\dfrac{-5}{2x^2} + C$)

e $-6x^{-1} + C$ (or $-\dfrac{6}{x} + C$)

f $\dfrac{x^4}{4} + x^2 + C$ **g** $2x^3 - x^5 + C$

h $\dfrac{x^4}{4} - \dfrac{1}{2x^2} + C$ **i** $x - \dfrac{1}{2x^2} + C$

j $\dfrac{-1}{x} - \dfrac{1}{x^2} - \dfrac{1}{3x^3} + C$

3 **a** $\dfrac{2}{5}x^{5/2} + C$ **b** $\dfrac{9}{5}x^{5/3} + C$ **c** $\dfrac{2x^{3/2}}{3} + C$

d $4x^{1/2} + C$ **e** $2x^{7/2} - 2x^{5/2} + C$

f $\dfrac{x^2}{2} + \dfrac{4}{3}x^{3/2} + x + C$ **g** $\dfrac{3x^{5/3}}{5} - \dfrac{2x^{3/2}}{3} + C$

h $\dfrac{2x^{5/2}}{5} + \dfrac{4}{3}x^{3/2} + 2x^{1/2} + C$

4 **a** $\dfrac{1}{2}e^{2x} + C$ **b** $\dfrac{-1}{2}e^{-2x} + C$ **c** $-12e^{-x/2} + C$

d $\ln x + C$ **e** $\dfrac{x^2}{2} - 2\ln x + C$ **f** $\int (1 + e^x)^2 \, dx$

$= \int (1 + 2e^x + e^{2x}) \, dx$

$= x + 2e^x + \dfrac{1}{2}e^{2x} + C$

5 **a** $\displaystyle\int_0^2 x^4 \, dx = \left[\dfrac{x^5}{5}\right]_0^2 = \dfrac{32}{5} - 0 = \dfrac{32}{5}$

b $\displaystyle\int_1^0 (x^3 - x)\,dx = \left[\dfrac{x^4}{4} - \dfrac{x^2}{2}\right]_{-1}^0$

$= 0 - \left(\dfrac{1}{4} - \dfrac{1}{2}\right) = \dfrac{1}{4}$

c $\displaystyle\int_0^1 e^{-x} dx = \left[-e^{-x}\right]_0^1 = -e^{-1} - (-1) = 1 - \dfrac{1}{e}$

6 Area is $\displaystyle\int_2^4 (x^2 + 4)\, dx = \left[\dfrac{x^3}{3} + 4\,x\right]_2^4$

$= \left(\dfrac{64}{3} + 16\right) - \left(\dfrac{8}{3} + 8\right)$

$= \dfrac{80}{3}$

7

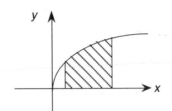

Area is $\displaystyle\int_1^4 x^{\frac{1}{2}} \, dx$

$= \left[\dfrac{2}{3}x^{\frac{3}{2}}\right]_1^4$

$= \dfrac{16}{3} - \dfrac{2}{3} = \dfrac{14}{3}$

8 We want

$\displaystyle\int_2^3 \dfrac{1}{x^2} \, dx = \int_3^x \dfrac{1}{x^2}\, dx$

$\Rightarrow \left[-\dfrac{1}{x}\right]_2^3 = \left[-\dfrac{1}{x}\right]_3^k$

$\Rightarrow -\dfrac{1}{3} + \dfrac{1}{2} = -\dfrac{1}{k} + \dfrac{1}{3}$ $\Rightarrow \dfrac{1}{k} = \dfrac{2}{3} - \dfrac{1}{2} = \dfrac{1}{6} \Rightarrow k = 6$

Section 10

1 $A_{MAX} = 3.75$ $B_{MAX} = 7.25$

   $A_{MIN} = 3.65$ $B_{MIN} = 7.15$

   a   max of $A + B$ is $A_{MAX} + B_{MAX}$

      $= 3.75 + 7.25 = 11.0$

      min of $A + B$ is $A_{MIN} + B_{MIN}$

      $= 3.65 + 7.15 = 10.8$

   b   max of $B - A$ is $B_{MAX} - A_{MIN}$

      $= 7.25 - 3.65 = 3.6$

      min is $7.15 - 3.75 = 3.4$

   c $A_{MAX} \times B_{MAX}$ $= 3.75 \times 7.25$

      $= 27.2$ (1 d.p.)   MAX

      $A_{MIN} \times B_{MIN}$ $= 3.65 \times 7.15$

      $= 26.1$ (1 d.p.)   MIN

   d $\dfrac{B_{MAX}}{A_{MIN}} = \dfrac{7.25}{3.65} = 2.0$ (1 d.p.)   MAX

      $\dfrac{B_{MIN}}{A_{MAX}} = \dfrac{7.15}{3.75} = 1.9$ (1 d.p.)   MIN

2 **a**   Since adding, we add absolute errors:

   Maximum magnitude is $0.05 + 0.05 = 0.1$

   b   If the error in p is 0.05, the error in $3p$

   is $3 \times 0.05 = 0.15$

   So the error is $3 \times 0.05 + 2 \times 0.05 = 0.25$

   c   The error is the *same* as for **b**, you always
   add the absolute errors, even when subtracting.
   Answer is 0.25.

3 **a**   Since multiplying, we add the relative
   errors, which is then $2 \times 0.5\% = 1\%$

   b   Since the relative errors in s and t have the
   same maximum value, the required error is

   again $2 \times 0.5\% = 1\%$

   c   Although dividing, we still add the
   relative errors.

   In total we have $2 \times 0.5\% + 1 \times 0.5\% = 1.5\%$.

4 **a** $f(0) = -4$, $f(1) = -11$, $f(2) = -12$,
      $f(3) = -1$, $f(4) = 28$

      Root is between 3 and 4

   b $f(1) = -3$, $f(2) = -1.3$, $f(3) = 0.1$

      Root between 2 and 3

   c $f(1) = -4.3$, $f(2) = 1.4$

      Root between 1 and 2

   d $f(0) = -3$, $f(1) = -0.3$, $f(2) = 0.8$

      Root between 1 and 2

5 Suppose $f(x) = e^x \cos 2x - 1$.

   $f(0.4) = 1.039 - 1 = 0.039$

   $f(0.45) = 0.975 - 1 \qquad = -0.025$

   Change of sign between two values of x so
   there is a root between them as required.

6 $(x + 1)^5 = (x + 2)^3 + 4$

   i.e. $(x + 1)^5 - (x + 2)^3 - 4 = 0$

   Suppose $f(x) = (x + 1)^5 - (x + 2)^3 - 4$

   Then $f(0.8)$ $=$ $18.896 - 21.952 - 4$

            $=$ -7.056

         $f(1)$ $=$ $32 - 27 - 4$

            $=$ 1

   Change of sign, so root between 0.8 and 1.